Transforming the
NATIONS

ADVANCING THE KINGDOM IN THE
MARKETPLACE AND LEADERSHIP

Dr. Leah Miracho

Book Cover by Brenda DeVries
Fonts: Baskerville, Avenir Next, Holiday Script
Cover image: shutterstock

First published in the United States in 2024
by Amazon Kindle Direct Publishing

ISBN: 9798344789088

www.kingdombusinessleadershipglobal.com

ENDORSEMENTS

It is an honor for me to endorse Dr. Leah Miracho's excellent book, *Transforming Nations: Advancing the Kingdom in the Marketplace and Leadership.* This book gives the reader practical solutions and incredible insights into how a combination of marketplace strategies, effective leadership and entrepreneurship (within the context of a broader spiritual awakening) can brilliantly transform nations for God. Leah has truly gifted us with a profound understanding of the heart and mind of God for the 21st century Church. She challenges both marketplace leaders and church leaders alike to demonstrate the Kingdom of God and transform their areas of influence. The reader will discover a divine transformational blueprint that only Holy Spirit could reveal. It is a must-read!

— Stacey Campbell, Founder of Shiloh Global
www.wesleyystaceycampbell.com

In Matthew 28:19, Jesus commissioned His disciples to "go and make disciples of all nations," defining this as "baptizing them in the name of the Father and of the Son and of the Holy Spirit," in other words to ready them for fulfillment of the prayer He had taught them about bringing the Kingdom of God "to earth as it is in Heaven (Matthew 6:10)." Although we have the authority of Jesus and walk in the power of the Holy Spirit, this is no easy task. In her book, *Transforming the Nations: Advancing the Kingdom in the Marketplace and Leadership*, marketplace minister and leader Dr. Leah Miracho examines many of the tools Jesus gave us to carry [this commission] out within our spheres of influence as businesspeople. The result is a highly readable call to action.

A walk through the Table of Contents reveals the scope of the book, covering a wide range of Kingdom issues from Business as Mission to Apostolic Authority to Kingdom Principles in Business to Strategies for Spiritual Mapping to Intercessory Prayer, and much more. Miracho draws on her own experiences, from growing up in a faith-filled, service-oriented family in Nairobi, Kenya, to her more recent practice as a software accounting engineer and project manager in Dallas, Texas, in addition to Biblical illustrations, offering practical insights to help each of us develop our own "how to" as we endeavor to fulfill The Great Commission. This book will prove to be a valuable resource for the body."

— Walt Pilcher, author of The Five-fold Effect:
Unlocking Power Leadership for Amazing
Results in Your Organization

Transforming the Nations: Advancing the Kingdom in the Marketplace and Leadership by Dr. Leah Miracho is an inspiring book focused on encouraging and empowering Christians in the Marketplace to thrive, advance, and prosper God's Kingdom in the sphere of economics. This work is a comprehensive strategic plan for Christian economic action and entrepreneurial endeavors. This book is a must read for Christian business people and Church leaders.

— Dr. Rob Covell, Provost
Wagner University

Dr. Leah Miracho has given leaders in the marketplace a book to help increase their influence, better manage their workplace, and live a life of intimacy with God that will yield the greatest impact on culture. The theory and practicality contained in this book will challenge you to go deeper in the things of God.

I highly recommend this book to anyone who desires to enrich, enhance and positively impact the workplace and region in which they live. Well done, Leah!

— Apostle Sharon Billins
Palm Tree International Ministries

DEDICATION

I dedicate this book to our Lord Jesus Christ. This has been a dream come true! And to my family, my father, mother, and my siblings who, by example, nurtured my leadership gift and saw that I was equipped to embrace and thrive in an evolving global landscape. Their love, encouragement, insights, and constant willingness to engage in thoughtful conversation were life giving in this challenging endeavor. My hope and desire is that my generation will live as reformers who bring significant transformation to the nations.

ACKNOWLEDGEMENTS

I want to acknowledge all who were essential in helping in the journey of writing this book. That includes those alive on the earth, and those who have already accessed Heaven. I would like to acknowledge my father, James, mother, Lucy, and my grandfather, Steven for their positive influence in my formative years as living examples of what it means to practice business as mission.

I would also like to express my deepest appreciation to Dr. Peter Wagner for serving as an apostolic forerunner who has championed the body of Christ in their call to take up their positions of cultural influence, and to Dr. Priscilla Hernandez. I am thankful to these individuals for their constant push to dig deeper into myself, for guidance, insightful feedback, and intellectual rigor that have been instrumental in shaping this work.

I would also like to acknowledge the support of my mentors whose expertise and suggestions were pivotal in refining the arguments and methodologies expressed in this book.

Lastly, I am deeply grateful to my family and friends for their constant support, understanding, and belief in my abilities.

Without their encouragement, this journey would not have been possible.

TABLE OF CONTENTS

Chap 11: Tech Kingdom

FOREWORD

The book you are about to read is an incredible resource for Kingdom entrepreneurs today, and will help pull you forward into your apostolic call and destiny in the marketplace.

I have enjoyed reading Leah's book and would have loved to have had a resource like this when I was starting my first business! Many business leaders were just learning about their call in the marketplace when I started my business. We were also just beginning to grasp the idea of the gospel of the Kingdom, not just salvation. It was a steep learning curve with just a handful of us sorting it out together. We didn't really understand it or know what to do, but we knew we were called to business.

The first time I heard confirmation of my call was from Os Hillman when he said we are all in full-time ministry wherever we are! That was my confirmation to continue on my quest to bring God and His Kingdom into everything I was doing in the marketplace. I learned a lot of things the hard way as a forerunner often does. What does this look like? How does this really work? How do I know I am doing right? How does planning and faith work together? What business practices did we learn in our educational process that do or don't apply to building a kingdom business? How do we bridge the gap with our employees and our faith without creating human resource issues?

The only thing I really knew was to stay in prayer, seek the guidance of the Holy Spirit, and stay in the word of God. It was in that place that God showed up and directed me through the above questions and unknowns. Did I do it all correctly? No! Did I make mistakes? Yes, so many. But did I press on toward the goal? Absolutely. It's our faith in God that keeps us moving when the world and the circumstances we can see don't look so promising. A prophet coach of mine always said, "Just keep looking up". And that's what I did. I also read everything I could find, explored many avenues, and continued educating myself in the word and in business.

Leah does a great job of covering so many of these questions and unknowns in her book. She covers both the idea of business and Kingdom principles, and how they can work together to bring forth influence and change culture. Leah also talks about our leadership responsibility, and characteristics we should implore as apostles in the marketplace.

We may be called to start our own business in which we can implement these leadership characteristics, but we also may be called to carry these leadership characteristics into other companies, and leadership positions in other non-business areas of influence in our culture.

Our business acumen is key, but our leadership characteristics are also key to bring influence and change into other areas of society; education, government, media, the arts, church, family, and of course business. Just looking at these areas of influence and culture today we can see the missing component of not only servant leadership, but apostolic leadership and Kingdom solutions!

Every area of influence needs to be impacted with these key Kingdom and apostolic leadership characteristics in order to shift these areas of influence into the nature and culture of heaven. Many have stated over the years that the apostolic and Kingdom movement in the marketplace will be key to bringing transformation there, and carrying it into all the other areas of influence. Leah speaks to this in her book as well, and I wholeheartedly agree!

As we all learn our call and position ourselves before the Lord, we can shift the marketplace and every area of culture and bring about sheep nations for God. What a great call and great responsibility. We must do it together with God and with each other as the Ekklesia operating in their skills and giftings in business and in every area of society.

— Dr. Wende Jones, Marketplace Apostle and President
of Apostolic Network for Kingdom Congressional
International Alliance

CHAPTER 1

TRANSFORMING THE NATIONS: ADVANCING THE KINGDOM IN THE MARKETPLACE AND LEADERSHIP

"From infancy you have known the holy Scriptures, which are able to make you wise for salvation through faith in Christ Jesus. All Scripture is God-breathed and is useful . . . so that the man of God may be thoroughly equipped for every good work."

2 Timothy 3:15-17

The ceiling has lifted! A new-sound movement of Marketplace Apostles and Prophets and other five-fold offices running together has begun! In an increasingly interconnected global economy, the marketplace serves as a powerful catalyst for national transformation. This book explores the multifaceted role of the marketplace in redefining a nation across various mountains of influence, which includes business, education, politics, religion and media markets. It highlights how market-driven strategies, effective leadership, and entrepreneurship can bring transformative and reformational strategies to guide a nation.

Like so many Christians, I grew up with misunderstandings about how the church is supposed to work, and that work can be ministry. I believed that work as ministry meant only working in a church, and that you had to be highly religious or spiritual to be found worthy of serving God. All I could see for this type of profession was constant preaching in the pulpit. I missed the fact that our everyday work can be a form of worship to God. This means that wherever I work, whether in business, healthcare, education, or any other field, I am ser-ving God by doing so with excellence, integrity, and for the audience of one.

The issue is that while we have been looking, we have not been seeing all there is to discover. Because we have looked through religious lenses, we have not seen the marketplace, much less its great importance to the God's Kingdom By broadening our perspective beyond just religious lenses, we're starting to recognize that we are not only discipling individuals within the church, we have missed the higher prize of bringing transformation to nations.

It's now a perfect moment that we put on Kingdom of God mindset that will allow us to see the Church operating 24/7 in the marketplace. This will help us identify our real objectives, identify the challenges, and to see the integration of all that empowers us to effectively disciple nations.

I now realize that all work is an opportunity to walk in His attributes. Isn't it exciting that we can honor God and bring glory to Him through all professions? It is my desire that a de-eper awareness would awaken and come alive within the body of Christ through this following exploration of the Kingdom in the marketplace and leadership. It is my sincere belief that our faith can have a tremendous influence and can even transform our professional environments, which leads to a more profound impact on society, corporate culture, industry standards, and even national development. In this book you'll learn key areas of focus, and receive practical applications wh-ich include ethical decisions making, and leadership strategies with the ultimate goal of fostering a transformative impact in the marketplace.

Here in the early 21st century, the traditional Christian church is in a drastic transition as it fights to remain relevant and influential in today's post-modern world. The problems it faces stem from man-made traditions, old, inaccurate theology, and the world becoming a seemingly darker place. One of the greatest challenges it faces is the way it sees itself in relation to -the world. While there has been some integration of the church into the workplace where we see Christians using their God-given skills in the world, there is still so much more that we can understand about our impact on the world when we realize that God designed us to do all kinds of different work.

God created man from the beginning of creation to give him dominion over the earth. It all began in Genesis. Then in the New Testament, we see that Jesus paid the price of reconciling us back to the Father, which allows the Kingdom to be established in us as we exercise the full authority He gave us here on earth. He died to give us back our true identity in Him, which was initially lost at the fall in the Garden. The first thing that God said to Adam and Eve was, "Be fruitful, and multiply, and replenish the earth, and subdue it: and have dominion over [all the creation]." (Genesis 1:28, NKJV) We must not miss the significance of this statement.

I like the idea that people are appointed as kings to rule the creation, knowing that we do so as a reflection of God himself. This book explores how nations can leverage the power of the marketplace to bring about profound and lasting transformation in our world.

It's time for Ekklesia to transition and manifest in the marketplace. We need to stop rolling up our rapture rugs to escape, and instead roll up our sleeves and take authority and rule over this earth as long as we are in it. We are to exer-cise the authority of the kingdom by revealing Jesus, occupying our places of authority until He returns! Yes, we cannot afford to waste time trying to ride escapist eschatology, waiting for Jesus until he comes.

It's like the story of the servant who buried the talent in Matthew 25:18. It's time for the church to walk in the Kingdom mindset, multiply, and bear fruit. We must occupy every sphere of society, influence, and advance His Kingdom on earth. We are the beacon of light in the earth.

In this book we will be covering the following topics: Adopting Business as a Mission, Learning to Hear the Voice of God, Mission and Apostolic Authority, The Great Wealth Transfer, Exercising Spiritual Mapping, and Applying Kingdom Principles in the Marketplace. These are some of the keys to unleashing Christian business leaders.

CHAPTER 2

BUSINESS AS A MISSION

Business as a mission is one of my favorite subjects. As someone who works in the marketplace, I apply Kingdom principles in my workplace. My work involves implementation of a new accounting process, changing systems, and giving new solutions. I daily depend on unpacking God's wisdom and strategic thinking about how to implement and change the systems within my line of work. Every day, I consult God for new ideas.

As the *Ekklesia* (the Greek word for Church) in the workplace, through the help of intercession we find ourselves confronting and conquering the seventh mountain of cultural influence–the Mountain of Business, which is one of the seven mountains mentioned by Lance Wallnau in his book, *7 Mountains: The Rise and Fall of Nations*. By sharing my own family history and personal experience, I illustrate how intimacy with the Lord is the foundation of everything.

Please note that throughout this discussion, the capitalized version of "Church" is used when referring to this New

Testament model; and "church" is used for general references to Christian denominations.

Dr. Peter Wagner explores this subject by addressing possible solutions to closing the gap between the traditional church rule book and business culture. God calls people into business for His purpose, and to bring strategic solutions to a world in need of true leadership today. There is no separation between work and church, but a call to bring a peaceful coexistence of transformation within both. These business solutions maximize opportunities to represent Jesus among unreached peoples and places all over the world. The main goal is to bring the Kingdom to earth.

To give a little history, I grew up in an environment where my dad was an entrepreneur. We my-siblings and I got in-volved in our family business when I was fourteen years old. I enjoyed the work, and it developed a passion in me to follow in his footsteps today. I have learned, and am still learning the wise adoption of a healthy workplace culture that intertwines both traditional and business culture rules that align with the Kingdom to bring transformation. Creating a healthy culture means pulling the vast resources of heaven that are available in the Kingdom toward our everyday lives, which affects how we function as stewards across all seven of the cultural mountains of influence.

Joseph, raised in a family wrought with strife and jealousy, had dreams and visions of being a leader in his family. In his dream, he saw himself in a position of leadership with his father, mother, and brothers bowing down to him. As part of the fulfillment of that dream, Joseph, through God's divine revelation, interpreted Pharaoh's dream whose imagery foretold an upcoming seven years of plenty followed by seven years of famine. This placed Joseph in a position of favor and administration with Pharaoh. His leadership roles were numerous and multifaceted.

DANIEL - The Book of Daniel
ROLE: High-ranking Official in Babylon and Persia, Interpreter of Dreams and Visions, Wise Counselor, Administrator, Advisor of Kings

MARKETPLACE INFLUENCE: Daniel served in the courts of four kings: Nebuchadnezzar, Belshazzar, Darius, and Cyrus of both the Babylonian and Persian empires. He navigated the complexities of these kingdoms without compromising his faith in God amidst challenges. His integrity, unwavering faith, exceptional wisdom, and prophetic insight influenced the policies and decisions of these empires making him a model leader.

Dr. Wagner writes in his book, *The Church in the Workplace*, that teaching on the differences between the Greek mindset and the Hebrew mindset was first popularized in apostolic and prophetic circles in 2018 by Chuck Pierce, the founder of Glory of Zion Ministries. The Greek mindset includes the belief that human beings, not God, are supreme. Greek ways of thinking separate things into well-defined categories.

The Greek mindset is human-centered, which results in humanism. The Hebrew Mindset is God-centered, which results in theism. Truth, for Hebrews, does not emerge from mere human reason, but comes from the revelation of God. Greek thought stresses knowledge, or proper thinking, while Hebrew thought stresses practice, or proper living.

In the Greek mindset, people try to pull the cards on how to achieve perfection through their own strength. The adoption of this mindset may be the reason many leaders seek man's approval, acceptance, and affirmation through performance. On the other hand, the Hebrew mindset has a God-centered approach, which acknowledges that all areas of life are sacred, and therefore sees marketplace involvement as being equally sacred as religious practices. This mindset retains the fact that God wants us to approach work as He first intended.

"On the seventh day God had finished his work of creation, so he rested from all his work. And God blessed the seventh day and declared it holy, because it was the day when He rested from all his work of creation." (Genesis 2:2:3)

Dualism emphasizes the sacred versus secular, and separates existence into two levels: the lower level of the physical world, and the upper level of the spiritual world. C. Peter Wagner expresses that the theory states that,

"The marketplace was 'carnal' because it dealt with 'earthly things' like business and money. Adultery was properly viewed as sinful, but the worldly realm of economics was viewed, like politics, as some kind of 'neutral zone' where Christianity had no real place trying to affect the system of economics, production, management, or distribution."

Dualism has greatly impacted traditional Christian culture with the concept that life is divided into secular and sacred, and seeks the disconnecting of the spiritual and seven spheres, where truth can be found. This includes the traditional separation of the clergy and laity. Wagner states, "The Postmodern church is an army that moves out into the battlefield, marshaled against the forces of the enemy, with divine assignment to retake the dominion of society, which Satan usurped from Adam."

WORK AND WORSHIP

Along with the God-centered mindset, another way to intertwine church and work is seeing work as worship. The Church in the Marketplace operates from a place of depending on the Father, Jesus, and Holy Spirit, to guide and help build heavenly strategies, and to bring a spiritual atmosphere to the workplace.

The Hebrew mindset helps professionals see from the heavenly place. This means that even in our professions we partner with heaven to restrain evil. Just as a king inherits and occupies their father's kingdom, we are also to occupy every territory and see how they are impacted by the Kingdom of God. God is constantly dispensing to us divine power, authority, and grace to co-labor with him in restraining Satan's evil operations.

God's children will solve problems, and overcome difficulties, obstacles, and troubles in all areas of life—including in the workplace. Paul instructs us, "Do not be overcome by evil, but overcome evil with good." (Romans

12:21) Our involvement in the marketplace is a part of our worship to Him.

CHAPTER 3

WHAT IS THE MARKETPLACE?

The marketplace is a corporate kingdom where people come to work and trade. Historically, it's been an open space market in a town, city, or country where people congregated for exchanges of merchandise and services.

These open spaces, mentioned in Matthew 11:16 and 20:3, Acts 16:19 and 17:17, as well as Luke 7:32, were not only used to put goods and services on display, but also functioned as a public arena or broad street where assemblies and trials were held, and professions of law, government, education, and industry also operated.

"Wherever He entered, into villages, cities, or the country, they laid the sick in the marketplaces, and begged Him that they might just touch the hem of His garment. And as many as touched Him were made well." (Mark 6:56)

Even today where, thanks to the internet, the marketplace is now global in its reach, it remains a fundamental concept in economics, representing the arena in which the exchange of goods and services takes place between buyers and sellers. It serves as a mechanism for individuals to satisfy their wants and needs through voluntary transactions.

The defining characteristic of a marketplace is its ability to bring together buyers and sellers, facilitating the process of trade. The marketplace has long been recognized as a powerful force in shaping economies and societies. In recent years, there has been a growing acknowledgment of the significant impact that the marketplace can have on transforming nations. By harnessing the potential of the marketplace, countries can foster economic growth, create employment opportunities, and drive innovation.

Economic growth contributes to enhancing stability which promotes social justice and enables access to essential resources such as healthcare and education, thereby opening doors to unlimited, enhanced opportunities, improving the quality of life in a society, and generating more employment opportunities for individuals within that community. Increased financial provision will meet the needs of the population, which will improve their standard of living, and increase their ability to obtain resources, thereby benefiting everyone within their sphere of influence. All of these factors advance the Kingdom of God.

WHAT ARE KINGDOM BUSINESSES?

Kingdom Businesses are for-profit companies whose mission is the expansion of the Kingdom of God. Unlike mainstream bu-sinesses, the main purpose of business as a mission is not just to merely maximize profit, but to produce profitable so-lutions to the problems of people and the planet.

As Kingdom business owners, we walk in the life-giving business of authority and leadership. We learn to partner with God to bring Kingdom strategies that will be effective, and to operate under the governance, ordinances, and principles of God. With tenacity, we penetrate all spheres of influence without the fear of the "Pharisees of men"—even as Jesus fearlessly faced those religious authorities in his day.

Ken Eldred notes in his book, *God is at Work*, "Kingdom businesses are for profit commercial enterprises in the mission field of the developing world through which Christian business professionals are seeking to meet spiritual, social, and economic needs. Kingdom businesses come in many sizes and shapes."

One Biblical example of business as a mission can be found in the parable of the talents in the book of Matthew (25:14-29). In this parable, a master entrusts his servants with different amounts of money and expects them to use it wisely and diligently to produce a profit. The servants who invest and multiply the money are praised, while the one who hides the money is reprimanded. This parable illustrates the importance of stewardship, hard work, and taking risks in business.

WHAT IS A MARKETPLACE APOSTLE?

Marketplace Apostles are representatives of the Kingdom of God here on earth. Because of their heart for God, they impact and influence society beyond the four walls of the church. They bring transformative and reformational strategies to guide a nation. Their Kingdom strength and authority is demonstrated through the leadership and wisdom they display which makes them an asset to nations today.

Matthew 16:18-19 (NIV) says, "And I tell you that you are Peter, and on this rock, I will build my church, and the gates of Hades will not overcome it. I will give you the keys to the kingdom of heaven; whatever you bind on earth will be bound in heaven, and whatever you loose on earth will be loosed in heaven." Marketplace Apostles are like Peter, called to build His church.

A Marketplace Apostle understands that the authority and function of Ekklesia is fundamental to properly implementing what Jesus initiated in Matthew 16:18, which is the building of His Ekklesia on the "rock" of Peter. For example, Christians in the marketplace who operate in the gift of wisdom are successful in negotiations, are capable of dealing with staff conflict, and respond well in highly competitive environments.

In other words, as it says in Proverbs 21:20, "In wisdom's house, you'll find delightful treasures and the oil of the Holy Spirit. But the stupid squander what they've been given."

The call is for all Jesus' disciples to step into authority, look around our workplaces and neighborhoods, pray blessings for those around us which will allow the Holy Spirit to transform lives, to be present in ways that allow the gospel message of Jesus to be shared personally with others, and to make disciples of Jesus Christ.

As discussed by Lance Wallnau, Marketplace Apostles represent the Kingdom in the marketplace. Because the Kingdom marketplace mission is one of the hot topics that will rise up in the next few years, it is time to educate those who believe that the Religion Mountain is the only sphere of Christian influence on the opportunities of bringing Kingdom into the marketplace, so that both spheres come together in their mission to gather the great harvest.

God loves diversity, and he created us to be very diverse. All apostles and leaders may have the same spiritual gifts and yet be different at the same time. God is the master of uniqueness, and has appointed apostles over all seven spheres of cultural influence. We all have been given unique apostolic assignments with diverse skills that will bring glory to God.

We all have a role to play in advancing the Kingdom of God today. Darren Shearer shares similar views with Dr. Wagner and Ed Silvoso (author of *Transformation: Change the Marketplace and You Change the World* and *Anointed for Business: How to Use Your Influence in the Marketplace to Change the World*). In his book, *The Marketplace Christian: A Practical Guide to Using Your Spiritual Gifts in Business*, Shearer talks about the role kings and priests play in the marketplace, and puts emphasis on the connection between ministry, church, and the marketplace, and sees the marketplace as a place to share and spread the awareness of God, and is a perfect place where disciples of Jesus are made Disciples of Jesus, according to these authors, are those who share in His faith and lead people to His paths through their actions in the marketplace.

Now more than ever, there is no doubt, the marketplace needs Christians to occupy it. Christianity is not to be locked within the four walls of the traditional institution of the church. It should be working itself out where people live and work. We must represent Jesus in the marketplace to that end. We are transformed by Jesus to impact the marketplace with Kingdom of God vitality.

EXAMPLES OF MARKETPLACE APOSTLES

There are several biblical figures that exemplify this idea through their actions and influence in marketplace domains. The following are some notable examples:

JOSEPH - Genesis 37-50

ROLE: Prime Minister of Egypt, Dreamer and Interpreter, Advisor to Pharoah

MARKETPLACE INFLUENCE: Joseph rose to a position of sig-nificant authority in Egypt, managing the nation's resources during a time of crisis to bring divine economic order and build community. God put Joseph in Potiphar's home to teach him large-scale administration. His administrative skills and wisdom not only saved Egypt, but also preserved his own family and many others. He was also known for his prophetic dreams and ability to interpret the dreams of others, including Pharaoh.

NEHEMIAH - The Book of Nehemiah

ROLE: Cupbearer to the King of Persia, later Governor of Judah, Visionary and Planner, Builder and Organizer, Reformer, Administrator

MARKETPLACE INFLUENCE: Nehemiah, a great leader, used his position and influence to secure resources and support for rebuilding the walls of Jerusalem. God put Nehemiah in this position that taught him political hardball. As a leader, he had strong administration and implementation skills which allowed him to break down a vision into incremental steps for His community to follow. He sought after God, and was fully dependent on Him.

As a prayer warrior who spent days fasting and praying over God-given blueprints, Nehemiah's servant leadership and organizational skills were crucial in restoring the city's infrastructure and reconciling God's set-apart people. He finished the work that God sent him to do no matter what opposition he faced. His impact on Jerusalem was profound and led to reformation and spiritual healing for the nation.

ESTHER - The Book of Esther

ROLE: Queen of Persia, Courageous Advocate, Strategic Planner

MARKETPLACE INFLUENCE: Esther used her position as queen to intercede for and act as a self-sacrificing advocate on behalf of her people, the Jews, which prevented their annihilation. Her faith, courage, and strategic leadership were instrumental in preserving her nation. Her leadership left a lasting generational legacy that continues to bring a reformation for future generations.

LYDIA - Acts 16:14-15

ROLE: Successful Businesswoman; Seller of purple cloth, a luxury item in the ancient world

MARKETPLACE INFLUENCE: Lydia was a successful, wealthy businesswoman in Philippi who became a strong, strategic believer who financially and logistically supported Paul, his companions, and other Christian movements. Her home became a meeting place for early Christian fellowship and teachings which is indicative of her transformative influence in the early church in Europe. She serves as a role model for Christian business leaders, demonstrating how financial resources can impact and advance the Kingdom of God.

PRISCILLA AND AQUILA - Acts 18:1-3, 18-26
ROLE: Tentmakers, Mentors, and Teachers

MARKETPLACE INFLUENCE: This married couple were tentmakers by trade, and integrated their business with ministry to create a bi-vocational ministry, which provided them with economic independence. They worked extensively alongside Paul in supporting missionary work, establishing and strengthening the churches in various cities, including Corinth, Ephesus and Rome. Their tent workshop may have served as a hub for evangelism and discipleship.

They were also instrumental in teaching and mentoring Apollos, an eloquent speaker and knowledgeable teacher of the word. According to Acts 18:24-26, they trained Apollos in the ways of God. They both had a deep intimacy and understanding of God's Kingdom that brought a transformation to other leaders in the early church. Their model inspires Kingdom leaders to balance their marketplace and ministry efforts effectively.

CORNELIUS - Acts 10

ROLE: Roman Centurion, Catalyst for Change,

MARKETPLACE INFLUENCE: Cornelius was a high ranking off-icer in the Roman army who was known for his piety and generosity. Cornelius was a leader who received a vision from an angel who instructed him to go to Peter in Acts 10:3-6. We later see his encounter with Peter that led to the spread of the Gospel among the Gentiles, and demonstrated the diverse attributes of God that brought in a cultural paradigm shift that infiltrated first century society.

MATTHEW (LEVI) - Matthew 9:9-13

ROLE: Tax Collector, Author, Apostle

MARKETPLACE INFLUENCE: Before he became one of Jesus' apostles, Matthew was a tax collector. This position required strong financial skills, an understanding of commerce and trade, and significant interaction with the secular world. His background and understanding of the economic and social dynamics of first century society provided a unique perspective in his Gospel writings. We later see his transformation and promotion into his role as an apostle, and his work as a great author, which highlights him as a great role model of redemption.

APOSTOLIC LEADERSHIP

An apostolic leader is a servant-leader with the recognized gift and fruit of an apostle. Their ability to lead by example is a lifestyle that starts with the heart. Apostles carry the blueprint, the big picture, and higher authority to transform their spheres of influence.

At the heart of Apostolic Christianity is a passion for being a Church determined to fulfill the commission given by Jesus to "make disciples of all nations" (Matthew 28:19). We do this by planting New Testament Churches, training, and releasing large-capacity leaders, and bringing the whole priesthood of believers (that Peter refers to in 1 Peter 2:9) to a place of liberty and effectiveness. Leadership is, and always will be, one of the most significant keys in the Kingdom of God. Jack Welch, an icon of business leadership, states it this way, "Before you are a leader, success is all about growing yourself. When you become a leader, success should be all about growing others."

Apostolic Models build the Kingdom with a vision to lead others. The model acknowledges all the fivefold ministries. Paul says,

"And He Himself gave some to be apostles, some prophets, some evangelists, and some pastors and teachers, for the equipping of the saints for the work of ministry, for the edifying of the body of Christ, till we all come to the unity of the faith and of the knowledge of the Son of God, to a perfect man, to the measure of the stature of the fullness of Christ." (Ephesians 4:11-16)

This model was designed by God to demonstrate who He is. In the Bible, from Genesis to Revelation, every statement is personified in Jesus as the Word who became flesh and dwelt amongst us. The Bible says that we saw His glory, the glory of the only begotten of the Father, who is full of grace and truth (John 1:14). This is what we want to exemplify as we build the Apostolic Model.

EPHESIANS 4:11-16 MODEL

It has always been the Father's desire to use apostolic leadership to build up the Church's foundation. In today's world, the greatest model that reflects the heart of the Father is found in Ephesians 4:11-16 (see Fig. 1).

Reggie McNeal states in his book *A Work of Heart,* "Apostolic leaders tend to be more collegial than competitive, more community-focused than merely focused on the church culture agenda." It is time to wholeheartedly seek out those who are lost. We must be a part of our Father's business. "For the Son of Man came to seek and to save that which was lost" (Luke 19:10).

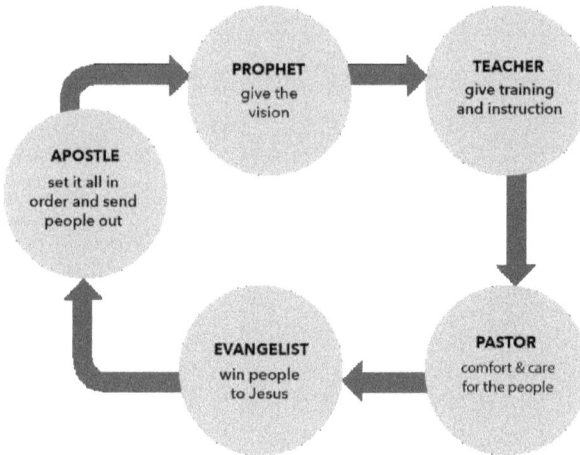

Figure 1: Ephesians 4:11-16 Model

Modern apostles desire to build by using the Seven Mountain Mandate to reshape the world system. They see the vision, and their desire is to create a blueprint for others to follow that will multiply their fruit. They flow in the creativity of the image of God as architect and builder. "See that you make all things according to the pattern shown to you on the mountain." (Hebrews 8:5)

They are like Nehemiah, who rebuilt the wall of Jerusalem during Judah's exile under the favor of Artaxerxes I of Persia. He understood the timing, purpose, strategy, who should build with him, and how to get the work done (the finishing anointing). Solomon was also one of the most extraordinary prototypes of someone who built with divine wisdom.

There was a prophetic element to the work and lives of Solomon, Moses, Nehemiah, and Abraham, and many other Biblical greats. An apostles' life is built with endurance. Every day, apostles are building for an eternal Kingdom. Knowing what and how to build through the Holy Spirit's revelation is one of the apostles' great pearls of wisdom.

The strength of a building lies in its foundation. The primary importance of the foundation is to hold the structure above it and keep it upright. According to construction experts and engineers, the foundation must withstand the "dead" load and "live" loads—the structural plus the variable—and likewise, modern apostles address both organizational needs and provide leadership for the people who are under their authority. The development process reminds us that Father God is the master builder. "Unless He builds the house, the builder labors in vain." (Psalm 127:1) From this foundation, an apostle can equip, impart, and establish people in the Kingdom!

The apostles advance the Kingdom by releasing fully equipped saints into their destiny. Apostles are those with an advanced understanding of the Kingdom-building process. They can hear what the Holy Spirit is saying to the Church, and build the right way at the right time. A mature apostle understands times and seasons (1 Chronicles 12:32, Daniel 2:21, Acts 1:7), and they effectively move with the Holy Spirit to build according to the heavenly pattern that's been given to them. (Exodus 25:40)

Peter Wagner highlights some main essential elements that comprise Apostolic leadership. Apostles have a spiritual gift to the Church and the Church's foundation.

"Now you are the body of Christ, and members individually. And God has appointed these in the church: first apostles, second prophets, third teachers, after that miracles, then gifts of healings, helps, administrations, and varieties of tongues." (1 Corinthians12:28-31).

The verse clearly lists them (apostles, prophets, evangelists, pastors, and teachers) in specific Kingdom government levels. It is interesting to see the same God-governed order flowing through the seven mountains—an area that has been overlooked and not affirmed by most believers.

Apostles have an assignment or call. They know where they are called and the purpose of their call. Their calling does not come with pride, but with humble obedience to God, and a willingness to act according to His will. They are willing to pay the price to fulfill their God-given Kingdom assignment, and carry a level of authority to lead and call forth things into existence. Because they live in the fear of the Lord, they treat others with honor and lead in reverence of Him.

To be truly effective in their call, apostles must have extraordinary character: blamelessness, humility, generosity, and passion. As C. S. Lewis said, "True humility is not thinking less of yourself; it's thinking of yourself less." Apostles are clothed with and walk in humility. They learn how to be humble through their submission to Father.

Some people with an apostolic gifting don't necessarily know where they're going. They need to be intimately connected in relationship with God to receive revelation from Him regarding direction. Effective apostles have a clear sense of vision which is received through spending time in intimacy with God, and then create and execute plans according to that vision. American novelist Ken Kesey explained, "You don't lead by pointing and telling people some place to go. You lead by going to that place and making a case."

The apostle's vision affects others. They bring this vision to life so that their followers can see the way ahead as they follow God's commands. They inspire others by helping to make the vision their own. They demonstrate this vision as part of their lifestyle.

The story of Joseph offers us some perspective on what an effective apostolic leader looks like. In Genesis 50:15-21, decades after they had sold Joseph into slavery, during a terrible famine, his brothers humbly went to him and bowed down to receive food that, through the revelation of Pharaoh's dream which God had given Joseph the ability to interpret. Joseph, as Pharaoh's second in command, had stockpiled in Egypt during prior years of plenty.

> "Joseph said to them, 'Do not be afraid, for am I in the place of God? But as for you, you meant evil against me; but God meant it for good, in order to bring it about as it is today, to save many people alive. Now, therefore, do not be afraid; I will provide for you and your little ones' And he comforted them and spoke kindly to them." (Genesis 50:19)

Joseph's character caused him to refrain from exacting vengeance on his brothers for selling him into slavery. While he was in Egypt, Joseph had spent time in God's character-building class. He used his power to bless his brothers rather than curse them.

Integrity is a crucial element of apostolic leadership that cannot be compromised. It is a fundamental prerequisite for ethical action. Some Biblical leaders often fail because they trade their integrity for earthly gain. I believe any leader with power and authority should walk in and exercise integrity at all costs. God has placed apostolic leaders in the marketplace for such a time as this because He knows the treachery of the day. Rise up and respond accordingly with the courage that is demanded to live a life marked by integrity.

The Apostolic Model is interested in ensuring that the Body of Christ brings God's wonder everywhere believers go. It challenges the world system of operations through prayer as the foundation, and sees God's Church as a living, growing organism—not as an organization.

Now, what does this look like in the Government Mountain? It is about advancing and taking dominion. We advance and take dominion on the mountain of Government by shaping the future of the nation and upholding Kingdom principles. Dominion involves using one's influence and power to enact Kingdom principles, promoting a system of righteous judgment, transparency, and exhibiting integrity and accountability in leadership, and upholding values of democracy and justice, establishing a strong foundation that impacts the well-being of constituents.

The core scriptural foundation for dominion is Matthew 28:19-20, "Go therefore and make disciples of all the nations, baptizing them in the name of the Father and of the Son and of the Holy Spirit, teaching them to observe all things that I have commanded you; and lo, I am with you always, even to the end of the age." In Genesis 1:26-28, we read, "Then God blessed them, and God said to them, 'Be fruitful and multiply; fill the earth and subdue it; have dominion over the fish of the sea, over the birds of the air, and over every living thing that moves on the earth.'" God gives man stewardship over the earth.

God's plan from the very beginning was that He would govern the earth through humans. God commanded Adam to take dominion. Our mandate is to establish a government on earth as if it is in heaven. Satan's purpose is to usurp the dominion over the world God had given to Adam.

In the Kingdom, apostles work together. Ekklesia becomes a powerful force when they work on their designated mountains of cultural influence, and bring strategic solutions from heaven to earth. Apostles lead the Ekklesia on how to take on their authority. Apostles carry God's vision for the nation. As long as apostles walk in the right motives through prayer, we will see citizens committed to God's purposes for government because those in authority bring His alignment and order.

In Romans 13, the Apostle Paul says that submission to governing authorities is instituted by God and is vested with legitimate authority. Everyone is subject to authority. Let every soul be subject to the governing authorities.

"For there is no authority except from God, and the authorities that exist are appointed by God. Therefore, whoever resists the authority resists the ordinance of God, and those who resist will [a]bring judgment on themselves. For rulers are not a terror to good works, but to evil. Do you want to be unafraid of authority? Do what is good, and you will have praise from the same. For he is God's minister to you for good. But if you do evil, be afraid; for he does not bear the sword in vain; for he is God's minister, an avenger to execute wrath on him who practices evil. Therefore, you must be subject, not only because of wrath but also for conscience's sake. Because of this, you also pay taxes, for they are God's ministers attending continually to this very thing. Render therefore to all their due: taxes to whom taxes are due, customs to whom customs, fear to whom fear, honor to whom honor." (Romans13: 1-7, NKJV)

Paul offers a very practical way for us to apply our beliefs by submitting to the God-given authorities, which includes leaders in government, the marketplace, and the church. Human beings flourish in a context of order and cooperation. He encourages leaders to build a society and bring peace to prosper within them.

Government exists and has been given extraordinary powers by God to facilitate such an environment. Government is a gift from God, and those who work and serve in it are worthy of honor and respect, and ought to be considered ministers of God, serving His purposes. We also see the five-fold at work in government.

Apostles carry a reforming mindset. They bring a visionary and pioneering spirit which brings transformation globally, locally, or regionally depending on the level of influence with which they've been entrusted. Prophets spearhead by bringing forth the vision and connecting people to encounters with God. The evangelist mobilizes and inspires citizens towards a common course. They bring the revelation of Jesus to those who don't know him. Pastors provide support, and cultivate the Kingdom character within the government, nurturing leaders by coaching or training them to be representative for him in office. Lastly, teachers bring forth biblical wisdom and knowledge through training to see the transformation by empowering decision-makers to make informed choices for the nations they represent.

Government may certainly fall short of its God-given ideal standard, just like any other organization or church, but that still does not negate that it is a gift from God that needs to be well stewarded. One of my favorite quotes from Dutch Sheets describes government as "God *is* government, He dele-gates a portion of His government, and Satan wants to usurp His government!" Isaiah 33:22 says, "For the Lord is our Judge, The Lord is our Lawgiver, The Lord is our King; He will save us." As Kingdom people, what should be our response? We step in and occupy. We become God's voice in the government.

Over the past year, we have seen startling revelations related to the powerful influence that the Chinese Communist Party (CCP) has built up in the United States. As Chuck Pierce of Glory of Zion Ministries recently said, "If things do not change, America will begin to look like China in the next few years. This is not in reference to the wonderful people of China, but rather the oppressive policies and surveillance state that the CCP inflicts on the people of China." "When the righteous are in authority, the people rejoice; but when the wicked man rules, the people groan and sigh." (Proverbs 29:2)

Godly reformation brings order rather than disaster, and brings complete alignment with Kingdom purpose and plans. Alice Patterson once said, "The foundation for apostolic building in government is prayer" and action. Through prayer, leaders take a stand and bring forth the strategies in the government.

Leaders who fear God, and are willing to do what it takes to see the will of the Father flourish in a nation instead of bringing destruction, understand God's desired outcome for that nation. We also see that a vision alone is not enough for an apostle to be effective in the Mountain of Government. Prayers are also their foundation. Apostles are called and equipped to shift structures with the church and with society in order to bring transformation.

Queen Esther stood in the king's inner court to mediate for salvation for a nation (Esther 4:10-17). She brought the vision to life. Moving with the power of the Holy Spirit in unity produces results. Apostolic leaders will inspire others by demonstrating the vision as a part of their lifestyle. When the righteous rule, the people of the land rejoice, but when the wicked rule, abominable acts bleed in the nation and government systems.

What we are facing in the United States today is the most advanced, aggressive, violent marginalization of society and the church that we have seen to date in our nation's history. Accepting the authority of the state over the church, the government has tried to establish a national religion. Stepping into our authority is one of the first acts of submission to God. We also see that there has been pressure to force submission to state mandates regarding public health and personal health issues.

We have seen the political ramifications of state authority. Abuse of authority is a critical issue that faces the church in America today. The way the government is run is a reflection of how people think and who (or what) they worship. The Kingdom of God will not advance until godly righteousness is established in our government. Apostles bring a fresh word into all spheres.

Politics are components that exist in any country that is governed under any form of leadership. Political Parties are organizations that have common ideologies and seek to gain influence in government by winning elections. Political parties function at each level of government: national, state, county, and precinct.

They are broken into two major groups and several minor groups. The two parties that hold the most influence in US politics are the Democrats and the Republicans. Each party develops a party platform, a statement of principles, and political philosophy that the party promises to enact if their candidates are elected to office. The platform assists voters in making election decisions, especially in a state like Texas, that has many elected officials, and no constitutional limit on how many terms a governor may serve. Parties also engage in fund-raising, candidate recruitment, and get-out-the-vote drives.

The participation of American citizens in any political process is anchored in the country's ideology that believes political engagement is a civic duty. This sense of civic duty encourages all American citizens to live up to their responsibility of having a clear understanding of the significance of the political system and how the government affects their lives. Thus, all American citizens are encouraged to support the government by participating in policy making and by complying with laws and regulations.

Laws that protect the public also have an effect on economic, social, and international relations, as well as other branches of political policy. According to Isaiah 9:7, "Of the greatness of his government and peace, there will be no end. He will reign on David's throne and over his kingdom, establishing and upholding it with justice and righteousness from that time on and forever. The zeal of the Lord Almighty will accomplish this." This scripture directly addresses legislation or law.

Every principle and every issue concerning earthly governments, and their politicians is stated in the Word. Every law enacted by those in governmental political jurisdictions is either moral, or immoral; righteous, or unrighteous; just, or unjust. Therefore, apostolic shepherds should not speak politically from the pulpit, but speak biblically regarding government and politics.

Apostolic leaders understand that the Kingdom of God is built on relationships, not only on ministry. They focus much of their time building key Kingdom relationships in informal settings that encourage the development of friendships. We see Jesus' objective was to get people to do things God's way, and, in doing so, replace human misery with human flourishing. This objective was to bring the Kingdom of God into all seven mountains of cultural influence.

With the nation's current state, it is good to say that we do not like what we see, and then take action to eradicate it. However, if we do not provide a viable alternative, something much worse could occupy the void. Apostles are called to give solutions. As Napoleon Bonaparte said, "The objective of war is victory, but the objective of victory is occupation." We must oust unrighteousness, but then we must occupy with righteousness. Jesus explained exactly what this should look like in his parable of the sheep nations and goat nations in Matthew 25.

What does it look like to have the Government of God operating in your city, community, or nation? The enemy is pressing hard to redefine culture, nations, and the identity of humanity. Part of his strategy has been to sideline the church, to block the flow of anointing, and to silence the church and cause it to retreat from being involved in government.

The nation is broken in so many ways, but the solutions will come from the sons and daughters of God. Every moral issue is a political issue. Every political issue is a moral issue. And every moral issue has a biblical solution. God has called sons and daughters with apostolic anointing to exercise dominion over society by taking authority over political and cultural institutions, to build and reshape the government system to reflect the Kingdom of Heaven.

Apostles have a Kingdom focus. They equip people, provide blueprints and plans for spiritual renovations, restorations, extensions, and constructions, and encourage people to occupy government positions, and send sons and daughters as representatives in government. In our current political state, redeemed democracy looks like many Kingdom-minded people working and having influence in all three (administrative, judicial, and legislative) branches of government to see the blessings of the Kingdom come on our country as God intended.

CHAPTER 4

HEARING THE VOICE OF GOD: MY STORY

In my earliest childhood memories, I remember being awakened daily to the sound of my mother in deep worship. Her morning love songs to Jesus saturated our home with an atmosphere of glory and life, like a daily alarm clock ushering us into a new day. There were occasions when my mother, Lucy, who was a prayer warrior, would shift into travail-warfare prayer at 3:00 a.m. The only quiet place where a mother of six could retreat was in her bedroom, and she would awaken the dawn with her worship.

As a young girl nestled in my bedroom with my twin and three sisters tucked into two bunk beds, my earliest memories revolved around a mother who prayed ceaselessly. Both of our parents were hardworking, God-fearing entrepreneurs who remained strong in their faith and family.

My mother was responsible for a household of eight where we lived in the capital city of Nairobi. She would sometimes come from her time with the Father with her face flushed bright red, like the swirling colors of an African sunset. Tears would cascade down her cheeks, and her eyes were red, almost like scars which were her trophies from her time spent in the presence of our family on her knees. She consistently met with her heavenly Father and taught us to meet with Him as well. She taught us how to inquire from God and listen closely.

THE SECRET IS THE SECRET PLACE

During special occasions, my mother would occasionally invite us children into her secret place of prayer. This occurred while my two older brothers were studying at Russian and German Universities. Unfortunately, there were no scholarships available at the time, so our family had to cover the cost of my brothers' education in Germany. Despite this, our family did not believe in hosting fundraisers, which was a common thing in our country.

One morning, my mother called upon the girls to join her in prayer for provision for our brothers' education. We trusted God to meet these needs, choosing to express gratitude to God in advance for how we believed He would answer our prayers, in line with His promises in the Bible. According to God's promises, when we ask for bread, He does not give us a stone (Matthew 7:9-11).

We expressed our gratitude to God in advance for the overflow, even before we saw Him answer prayers. Within a week of praying, our prayers were answered. My brother's tuition was paid in full. Afterwards, my mother gathered the girls to sit on her bed and to take into account what God had provided, after which we celebrated by dancing and singing.

My mother, Dr. Lucy, was a doctor who managed her own hospital in Kenya. Every time she would treat a patient, she would first ask if she could pray for their healing. Some patients experienced supernatural healing, and did not require further medical attention. She would recommend a holistic natural approach to healing—treating each and every patient's spirit, soul, and body.

Following our prayer, my mother attended to numerous patients within a week. Many of the patients voluntarily paid more than their medical bill to show their gratitude. Even patients without money are provided care, and instead exchange goods from their farms for medical treatment.

THE VALUE OF HARD WORK

My Father, James, was a dedicated businessman who left the house at 4:00 a.m. every day to work to provide for his family. He did not believe in merely working to build other people's dreams, or just working as an employee for someone else's company. As a man of unwavering faith, he encouraged my mother, who had been married to him over thirty years, to start her own hospital. If my mother was described as a woman of prayer, my father was characterized as a man of faith. He was a Marketplace Apostle who excelled in entrepreneurship.

My dad taught us the importance of hard work, the skills required to thrive in the marketplace, and the concept of doing everything unto the Lord. He was always willing to listen to our dreams, and then encouraged us to take practical steps to help us develop the character we would need to make our dreams come true.

From the time I was about ten years old, we accompanied our father to his workplace for a few hours each day. Over the years, he gradually increased our responsibilities, imparting to us the skills needed to manage the restaurant during our high school years. He instructed us in the proper handling of finances, and instilled in us the importance of investing wisely.

Every evening, my father made it a point for us to gather together as a family and discuss our day. He was always home in time for dinner, and made spending the evenings with his children a priority. He was like an African lion who is so protective over his cubs.

My dad was known in the community to be such a fierce protector, a man of no nonsense, and a devoted father! He would smile with his beautiful Kenyan, bright white grin, compassion pouring from his eyes. He would address each of us children directly, sharing his wisdom, asking thought-provoking questions, and offering valuable insights on how to become assets to society. His questions caused us to think. How can we each become productive citizens? How can we not depend on anyone, or on the government, and instead give back to the community rather than take from it? He emphasized the importance of becoming productive leaders with strong character, self-reliance, and integrity.

My father strongly believed in teaching through his own daily actions, and setting an example for us to follow. When my mother transitioned to be with the Lord, instead of simply giving us money as an inheritance, he personally instructed each of us in business investment. Even in the management of his restaurant we learned valuable business skills, and learned how to build a business with raw materials from the ground up. We understood the process of entrepreneurship from start to finish.

He aimed to instill in us an understanding of the importance of passing down wealth through generations. Because we grew up with a mother who was a nurse, my siblings and I attended medical camp, where both of our parents re-emphasized the importance of hard work and giving back to the community. Through carefully laid-out steps and daily efforts, we were able to establish a foundation of wealth within our family. My father exemplified the Parable of the Talents in Matthew 25:29: "For to everyone who has will more be given, and he will have an abundance. But from the one who has not, even what he has will be taken away."

HEARING GOD'S VOICE: MY EXPERIENCE

One beautiful early morning during my quiet time, I was filled with the profound presence of God while consulting with Him as I had been working on an exciting major project for a Fortune 500 company. I clearly received a detailed blueprint that outlined step by step instructions on how I was to execute this project. I recall feeling an unmistakable presence, and I would get download after download of ideas in my spirit. I found myself scribbling down all the things I was receiving.

The voice guided me through different scenarios of creative ideas, which allowed me to vividly envision the final solution. I was so grateful to God that he had joined me in this process. I faithfully implemented and executed these solutions, which resulted in a significant transformation of the revenue process, which in turn yielded a financial benefit of $4.1M in total realized revenue benefits which included revenue growth, improved working capital, and enhanced productivity through FTE savings.

The Bible also contains numerous accounts of leaders who encountered God and saw visions and dreams with implementable plans.

Examples include the following: Moses received the Ten Commandments (Exodus 19-20), Noah received instructions on how to build the Ark (Genesis 6:13-22), King David received detailed plan for building God's temple (1 Chronicles 28:11-19), God gave Gideon specific instructions on how to deliver Israel from the Midianites (Judges 6-7), Joshua received specific instruction on how to conquer the city of Jericho by marching around the city walls seven times (Joshua 6:1-5). Joseph received a dream from God that foretold his future leadership and rise in authority, and he also implemented a plan to store grain during seven years of famine, thus saving his family who would one day become

God's chosen nation, as well as the surrounding nations of his time (Genesis 41:37-57). I encourage you to choose to listen, hear from God when He speaks, and partner with Him.

BUSINESS AS MISSION CASE STUDY: MEDICAL CAMPS

Many marginalized communities face significant barriers to accessing healthcare. Medical camps are a means of bringing healthcare services directly to these communities where people are able to receive equitable care regardless of their socioeconomic status.

In collaboration with various healthcare organizations, non-profit organizations, and government agencies, my mother provided essential medical care to those who lack access to healthcare facilities. Medical camps act as an essential lifeline for individuals who would otherwise go without necessary medical attention. One critical reason for the importance of medical camps in Kenya is the substantial lack of access to healthcare facilities in rural and impoverished areas.

Many communities in Kenya are situated in remote areas with limited infrastructure which makes it challenging for residents to access medical care. Medical camps offer a solution by bringing healthcare services directly to these communities, which eliminates the barrier of distance and transportation cost. Additionally, a wide range of medical services, including primary care, dental care, eye care, immunizations, and health education, were provided.

This comprehensive approach ensured that individuals received the care they needed to address all kinds of various health concerns. Furthermore, we included screenings for chronic diseases such as diabetes, hypertension, and HIV/AIDS, which are all prevalent in Kenya. Early detection and treatment of these conditions can significantly improve health outcomes and prevent long-term complications.

In addition to providing medical treatment, healthcare professionals at these camps educated individuals on preventive measures, healthy lifestyle choices, and disease management. This holistic approach not only addressed immediate healthcare needs, but also empowered individuals to take charge of their own health and well-being.

Ultimately, medical camps play a crucial role in promoting preventative healthcare and early detection of medical conditions in Kenya, which contributes to improved health outcomes for individuals and communities. It is paramount that continued support and resources are allocated to these medical camps to ensure that all individuals have access to quality healthcare.

In today's world, Business as Mission models, as expressed in the example above, have garnered a great deal of attention. However, leaders of the nuclear church and those in parachurch businesses are not moving forward shoulder to shoulder. Leaders of both forms of the church must be open-minded, understanding, and appreciate where each group is coming from. "Going back to the minefields, if the church in the workplace is going to flourish and if God's people are going to transform society, the minefields must be cleared." Dr. Wagner continues, "I am confident that when Marketplace Apostles are recognized for who they are, we will see new strategies and actions that will result in major, beneficial changes in cities and nations in the world."

The spiritual gift of apostleship in the marketplace has great impact when authority and dominion are exercised in business culture. God's wisdom is the main resource for applying different business solutions such as negotiating, acquiring, leading, and implementing new processes, system automation, among others.

Because we have access to the resources of His wisdom, we are able to evolve with our Heavenly Father. Learning to adapt to change reignites the fire within us, and we become capable of transforming any atmosphere to operate according to His Kingdom principles. We use wisdom and creativity to acquire resources and wealth. Marketplace Christian leaders have become the bridge between the Kingdom of God and the world. They are the light of the world.

GODLY LEADERSHIP

Father, Jesus, and the Holy Spirit are our best prototypes for defining how we are to properly exercise leadership. We are to lead with love, humility, grace, and honor. This kind of leadership is universal, and not limited to any one nation. This is superior and respectful leadership.

We have also seen the eradication of the Babylonian economy. This means an eradication of social distress caused by greed, fear, corruption, and self-centeredness. This includes issues of poverty, homelessness, unemployment, starvation, trafficking, substance abuse, domestic violence, family breakdown, unsustainable debt, suicide, slavery, radicalization, abortion, unfunded liabilities, and the like.

We have seen different organizations like World Vision Christian Organization tackle global issues like ones discussed earlier in this book, replacing all these social dilemmas with a Kingdom culture of caring and sharing. This leads to universal prosperity and human flourishing.

These organizations are leading nations to have a superior economy that is built on a foundation of worship to the one true God. I know we are not fully there yet, but I can see that a huge shift in the marketplace is coming, where true leaders impact how the Kingdom of God looks on the earth.

I see a generation that is moving beyond mere citizenship and is beginning to invest their life resources in learning the loyal ambassadorial roles of Kingdom sonship. They are those who serve with integrity, dignity, and class as sons and daughters of God. God is shaping a new wineskin in the marketplace. The idea of a one-man show is diminished in the Kingdom. The resources from a successful Kingdom marketplace business will advance all who participate. Leaders are understanding, and are walking in the creativity of heaven. There is so much life of God in the marketplace.

THE FIVEFOLD GIFTS IN THE MARKETPLACE

Ephesians 4:11 (KJV) says, "And he gave some, apostles; and some, prophets; and some, evangelists; and some, pastors and teachers." These roles have always been part of God's original intent for how His Kingdom is to reach the entire globe.

The term *apostle* is derived from Classical Greek ἀπόστολος (*apóstolos*), meaning "one who is sent off", and is a term that is exclusively found in the New Testament. In the King James Version of the Bible, *apóstolos* can be found eighty-one times in eighty verses. In nineteen of these verses, "*apóstolos*" is defined as "a delegate, messenger, one sent forth with orders." This definition has consistently been applied to a religious delegate or messenger.

If you have received a vision, dream, passion, direction, or instruction from God to start your own business, then you can be considered a "delegate" or "messenger" who is "sent forth with orders." An apostle is the head of an organization, whether that be a ministry or a business. They have the ability to start something from nothing, bring people together for a specific purpose, and mentor and develop individuals into leaders with specific skill sets. Apostles understand and develop the big picture, or business plan, and also have the capacity to function in any other ministry or business office as well. This makes apostles excellent mentors.

Romans 1:1 (The Message) describes this leadership role by stating, "I, Paul, am a devoted slave of Jesus Christ on assignment, authorized as an apostle to proclaim God's words and acts." The purpose of an apostle is to inspire and encourage others to succeed, be it in business or in ministry.

Apostles are established apart from others, and serve as builders and leaders. They are delegates, messengers, and ones sent forth with orders. According to Romans 1:1 (The Message), the apostle is "a devoted slave of Jesus Christ on assignment, authorized as an apostle to proclaim God's words and acts." The distinct role of the apostle is more comprehensive than merely preaching the gospel. As the word of God divulges the guidelines for success in business or ministry, my belief that God calls individuals into business specifically for His purpose is affirmed.

Another function of an apostle in both ministry and business is that they multiply themselves by developing and elevating other leaders in an organized hierarchy of leadership under their authority. Indeed, an apostle develops a business or ministry to find, mentor, and train other individuals to preserve and broaden their vision. Particularly in the business context, there is indeed an organizational hierarchy, and in order for individuals to ascend, it is necessary for them to prove that they are capable of managing the responsibilities that come with apostleship, the highest level of which is the Chief Executive Officer (CEO), or President of the company.

While God may not have appointed individuals in the traditional sense of a ministry apostle, the marketplace offers an exceedingly fertile ground for ministry compared to the restricted environment of a church.

The term prophet in Ephesians 4:11 is derived from the Greek word prophet (προφήτης) and denotes "one moved by the spirit who speaks forth and discerns and foretells certain future events that are favorable to the Christian's cause." Prophets have distinct functions that are highlighted in the following passages from the Bible. One is forecasting or predicting the future:

> "And in these days prophets came from Jerusalem to Antioch. Then one of them, named Agabus, stood up and showed by the Spirit that there was going to be a great famine throughout the world, which also happened in the days of Claudius Caesar." (Acts 11:27-28)

Another is offering direction for the future:

> Now in the church that was at Antioch there were certain prophets and teachers: Barnabas, Simeon who was called Niger, Lucius of Cyrene, Manaen who had been brought up with Herod the tetrarch, and Saul. As they ministered to the Lord and fasted, the Holy Spirit said, 'Now separate to Me Barnabas and Saul for the work

to which I have called them.' Then, having fasted and prayed, and laid hands on them, they sent them away (Acts 13:1-3).

Finally, prophets oversee situations and provide correction if necessary. Acts 15:32 tells us, "Now Judas and Silas, themselves being prophets also, exhorted and strengthened the brethren with many words."

In essence, a prophet assumes a role akin to that of a CFO (Chief Financial Officer) or COO (Chief Operating Officer) in a business. This gift is indispensable for the financial stability and continued progress of any business, whether corporate or home-based. The words of a prophet necessitate rigorous testing to demonstrate their verifiability.

The assessors must evaluate the accuracy of their predictions, just as a CFO/COO who works with a CEO does. In terms of business, we see that a prophet's role in relation to an apostle is then similar to that of an auditor or an accountant's role in relation to a CEO. Paul says in 1 Corinthians 14:29 (KJV), "Let the prophets speak two or three and let the other judge." The remnant is finding and hearing the word, and finding their calling to adapt, function, and thrive in Kingdom business.

Those with the role of evangelist passionately share the good news of Jesus Christ. They often preach the gospel and announce glad tidings. *Evangelist* is derived from the Greek word *"euangelistes,"* which means "bringer of good news." In the business world, an evangelist can be compared to an advertiser, or someone in marketing who shares with potential customers or clients the things that are good about the products or services they are offering.

We have taken a look at how three of the five gifts (apostles, prophets, and evangelists) outlined by Paul function within the Church, and how those same gifts function in the marketplace. The remaining two, pastors and teachers, may appear to fall outside the focus of the marketplace discussion, but these gifts are much needed for Kingdom work in all spheres. Teaching gifts are also useful in business in the form of marketing and advertising. Marketers help teach the public why a particular product or service is useful.

The gift of pastor can be seen as salespeople or staff who are attentive and care for and create meaningful experiences for customers, guests, and/or clients. This can be seen especially in the industries of retail and hospitality.

CHAPTER 5

MISSIONS AND APOSTOLIC AUTHORITY

APOSTOLIC MARKETPLACE LEADERSHIP

What is dominion? Dominion is taking charge of something. It is the authority to subdue and control the resources of the Kingdom. Man was created to have fellowship with God, which leads to dominion. God gave man stewardship over His creation when He commanded Adam to take dominion in Genesis 1:26-28, "Be fruitful and increase in number; fill the earth and subdue it. Rule over the fish in the sea and the birds in the sky and over every living creature that moves on the ground." Our mandate is to establish a government on earth as if it is in heaven.

Dominion Mandate is the authority to command. Consider the Great Commission found in Matthew 28:19-20. "Therefore, go and make disciples of all nations, baptizing them in the name of the Father and of the Son and of the Holy Spirit, and teaching them to obey everything I have commanded you. And surely, I am with you always, to the very end of the age." Believers are the governing body of the

Kingdom of God, and are called by Him to administer Kingdom authority as His ruling ambassadors on this earth."

Dr. Wagner's definition of Dominion Theology is the practical theology that best builds on a foundation of social transformation, which is sometimes called "Kingdom now." Theology is a human attempt to explain God's word and His works in a reasonable and systematic way. Even though Jesus' Kingdom is, right now, established on the earth, we don't yet experience the fullness of God's Kingdom because we are still living within a redemptive timeline. God's Kingdom, because it is a Kingdom of spirit, exists beyond the boundaries of space and time.

The Kingdom of God is the spiritual realm over which God reigns as King, and is enacted through the fulfillment of God's will being done on earth. This glory realm, the heavenly dimension we have access to through Jesus because of His atoning sacrifice on the cross, is designed to be seen or experienced in the physical realm. Sons and Daughters of God have been given the authority to enjoy the benefits of operating from this Kingdom. "...and raised us up together, and made us sit together in the heavenly places in Christ Jesus." (Ephesians 2:6)

In most countries, any foreigner becomes a citizen through the process of naturalization. There is an allegiance to the land to which one seeks to become a citizen. Allegiance speaks to loyalty and love for the country, and a sense of belonging. There is a gradual growth of love for the country, and through acquired citizenship, one becomes entitled to the protection and privileges afforded a citizen.

There is a similarity between Kingdom citizenship and earthly citizenship. Only those who are willing to adhere to the process of the Kingdom of God will receive Kingdom citizenship. This process of becoming a citizen in the Kingdom of God is known as salvation that only comes through Jesus Christ. Citizenship is acquired through belief and acknowledgement of Jesus as savior and King.

> "Jesus answered, 'Most assuredly, I say to you, unless one is born of water and the Spirit, he cannot enter the Kingdom of God. That which is born of the flesh is flesh, and that which is born of the Spirit is spirit. Do not marvel that I said to you, 'You must be born again.' The wind blows where it wishes, and you hear the sound of it, but cannot tell where it comes from and where it goes. So is everyone who is born of the Spirit.'" (John 3:3-5)

Being born again in the Spirit lifts us beyond the earthly realm to the Kingdom realm. There are extraordinary benefits of being heirs of this Kingdom. The children of God gain resources, knowledge, and help to increase their sphere of influence in the glory of the King.

In the coming days, we will know and see this demonstration of the manifestation more and more. This generation will see the emergence of the Kingdom upon the earth when they gain the knowledge of their dominion by receiving their mandate. As the flame of His Spirit increases, the intensity of love for God and His Kingdom grows in the hearts of His children.

> "In the times of those kings, the God of heaven will set up a kingdom that will never be destroyed, nor will it be left to other people. It will crush all those kingdoms and bring them to an end, but it will itself endure forever. This is the meaning of the vision of the rock cut out of a mountain, but not by human hands—a rock that broke the iron, the bronze, the clay, the silver, and the gold to pieces. The great God has shown the king what will take place in the future. The dream is true, and the interpretation is trustworthy." (Daniel 2:44-45, NIV)

After interpreting King Nebuchadnezzar's dream, Daniel knew that it was the time of God's Kingdom on the earth—a Kingdom that would replace the devil's world system. When the stone not made with human hands shatters man's proud image, then the kingdoms of this world will become the Kingdom of our Lord and of His Christ. "Then the seventh angel sounded: And there were loud voices in heaven, saying, 'The kingdoms of this world have become the kingdoms of our Lord and of His Christ, and He shall reign forever and ever!'" (Revelation 11:15)

Dominion Theology has been one of my favorite teachings. I love exploring it with the Father, learning how to use it daily in the workplace, and applying the values that God would have me use, raising my work standard daily just as man was meant to tend and take care of the Garden in Genesis.

What does Dominion Theology look like in the marketplace? I am frequently asked that question. It looks like our spiritual gifts. For example, when Christians in the marketplace have the gift of wisdom, they will be very successful in negotiations, will be able to deal with staff conflict, and respond effectively in a highly competitive environment.

In other words, as it says in Proverbs 21:20 (TPT), "In wisdom's house you will find delightful treasures and the oil of the Holy Spirit. But the stupid squander what they have been given." The other gifts of the spirit are also instrumental in marketplace success:

> "For to one is given the word of wisdom through the Spirit, to another the word of knowledge through the same Spirit, to another faith by the same Spirit, to another gifts of healings by the same Spirit, to another the working of miracles, to another prophecy, to another discerning of spirits, to another different kinds of tongues, to another the interpretation of tongues." (1 Corinthians 12:8-10)

I acknowledge that having the spiritual gift of apostleship in the marketplace is my opportunity to exercise authority and dominion in business. The Psalmist also tells us, "You have made him to have dominion over the works of Your hands; You have put all things under his feet." (Psalm 8:6)

My calling and joy are to see and allow Heavenly Father to fully extend my dominance in the marketplace as I occupy the territory I've been given, knowing that God has given me the authority to govern all things entrusted to me for

His glory. I let go of my old mindset and acknowledge that I have the authority to govern what He has entrusted to me. I don't have to question my ability to be creative with witty ideas for my business. So many of us are often scared to excel or stand out, and we forget that we are blessed to exercise His dominion over the resources that have been given to us.

Based on Isaiah 61:3, Daniel 4:20-22, and Ezekiel 31, we can glean what we, as trees planted by the Lord, are supposed to resemble. We are planted with divine possibilities. Isaiah tells us we are "Oaks [trees] of Righteousness," "The Planting of the LORD," in order to display his splendor. In Daniel, we see:

> "The tree that you saw, which grew and became strong, whose height reached to the heavens and which could be seen by all the earth, whose leaves were lovely and its fruit abundant, in which was food for all, under which the beasts of the field dwelt, and in whose branches the birds of the heaven had their home—it is you, O king, who have grown and become strong; for your greatness has grown and reaches to the heavens, and your dominion to the end of the earth." (Daniel 4:20-22)

A generation is looking for authentic leadership found in the Kingdom of God. Who will listen to the marching orders given by God? He has planted everything we need inside of us. With this in mind, we often find ourselves facing the question, "What is the right way to do it?" and we expect that doing th-ings the "right way" will eliminate the need for our own creative input. Instead, we should be asking, "What is the best way to do things?" or even, "How can we do it better?" This allows us to increase in Godly maturity and partnership with him as Kingdom collaborators.

There's not always a one-size-fits-all answer to every problem. Jesus is our safe place for self-discovery. His sacrifice on the cross purchased our freedom to do what we are supposed to do.

PARADIGMS AND PARADIGM SHIFTS

A paradigm shift is a fundamental change in the way we process basic concepts and absorb information. Paradigms are our mental framework, and they play a crucial role in shaping our perception and understanding of the world.

It is evident that different people can receive the exact same information, but, because of their different perceptions, they interpret and utilize it in a variety of different ways. This is due to the fact that individuals have different paradigms. It is important to note that everyone operates under the influence of multiple paradigms, and this is particularly noticeable in politics.

For example, in a democratic society like ours, it can be confusing to witness Democrats and Republicans interpreting the same facts differently. Rather than assuming one party is right, and the other is wrong, it is wise to acknowledge that both may be correct in that they are both trying to make decisions and live their lives as ethically as possible based on their respective paradigms. We tend to align ourselves with those whose paradigms align with our own, which influences our support and voting decisions.

While our paradigms help us organize and make sense of our experiences, they also have the potential to limit or even restrict our comprehension, and impede our ability to acknowledge the workings of the Spirit of God. When we become too attached to a particular paradigm, it becomes a filter through which we view all spiritual experiences and insights. This can lead to narrow-mindedness and resistance to new ideas and ways of thinking. Instead of remaining open to the leadership of the Holy Spirit, we become fixated on maintaining our existing beliefs, rejecting any concepts that do not align with our paradigm.

Here is a good personal example of a paradigm shift as explained by a colleague of mine. She said that she was raised in a Calvinist Protestant Church. Within that denomination, they declared the Apostle's Creed which speaks of each member of the triune Godhead--Father, Son, and Holy Spirit. Though they spoke of the Holy Spirit, and though she had never encountered outright teaching on cessationism, which claims that the supernatural ministering gifts of the Holy Spirit no longer function in present day Christianity, her perspective was filtered through a paradigm of practiced cessationism.

"We didn't talk much about the Holy Spirit," she said, "and knew nothing about Holy Spirit baptism, and no one I knew operated in supernatural gifts of the Spirit. It wasn't until I was in college and after I had moved to Southern California that I began to encounter God in a whole different way. Through my encounters in the church, I experienced and saw people who were baptized in the Holy Spirit, and heard testimonies of people operating in supernatural gifts."

She expressed to me that she had always had a hunger for more though she could not pinpoint what was missing from her practiced faith--like there was something more that she may never have achieved in her lifetime.

When we were growing up, my mother took our family to revival meetings, and we experienced the Church that looked like the Church in Acts. What this woman had experienced was far from it. She realized that what she read in her Bible was not what she experienced in her day-to-day life.

"If I had embraced cessationism as my paradigm," she told me, "I would have missed out on so many more wonderful ways of encountering God." All of that being said, I wonder if there are others who, because they are "open minded" have, in their quest for what they understand to be truth, have abandoned Godly paradigms, and that which is really true?

It's good to search for the truth. And if we discover that we're believing something about God or life that isn't true, we should reject it. But many have been deceived or walked away from faith in Jesus using that same argument. And I would argue that they didn't really know the really real Jesus.

Moreover, paradigms can potentially sow discord and disagreement among believers as individuals become entrenched in their own perspectives and fail to recognize the worth of others' viewpoints. My colleague also offered this this example: "I'm pro-life," she said, "and I believe in the healing power of God, and in his provision to make ways that severely (if not completely) eliminate any reason for abortion to ever be an option with the paradigm that because we are image bearers of God, we all have a right to live in the fullness of that identity. To abort a fetus is to take a life.

However, someone who disagrees with me may argue for the case of abortion from their perspective of not understanding or embracing God's provision. Maybe they're concerned that they won't be able to care for another child, or maybe there are instances where it appears as though the mother's life may be in danger if a fetus is carried to full term. Through their paradigm, they may see abortion as an option of compassion for the mother--or maybe even for the child if it appears that it may be born with severe defects or abnormalities. They may see people who are hard and fast pro-lifers as being callous or unconcerned with the wellbeing of women.

My question to you is this: How do we begin to see one another through a lens of compassion so that we are able to open up to and engage in meaningful dialog and operate from a place of genuine love and care?

I feel like 'love' as defined in 1 Corinthians 13 is the plumbline. True believers in Jesus will be identified by these things that marked Jesus's own ministry: sacrificial *love* and *authority*--authority to live lives of integrity (delivered and free from bondages of sin), and authority to heal the sick, cleanse the lepers, open the eyes of the blind, cast out demons, raise the dead and operate in supernatural signs and wonders. And one more thing: Open declaration of the lordship of Jesus the Messiah."

To foster the Spirit of God, we must be prepared to challenge and broaden our existing paradigms. This demands humility, openness, and a willingness to embrace new ways of thinking and perceiving the world. By doing so, we can create room for the Holy Spirit to operate and influence our lives, leading us to a deeper understanding and unity with God and one another.

MINISTRY IN THE WORKPLACE PARADIGM

The most liberating paradigm shift is the shift from church vision to Kingdom vision. Ministry was not supposed to be limited within the four walls of the institutional church, or only on Sundays, but also in the workplace, Monday through Friday.

When we allow the Bible to speak to us about different professions in government, economics, education, science, art, communication, and business—what we may have traditionally considered to be the world systems and structures—we come to know that all of this belongs to our Heavenly Father. The job of sons and daughters is to be good and faithful stewards of everything they have been given. Because I've worked in the corporate world and the marketplace, I have learned to never leave Biblical values and principles outside the work office.

In Ephesians 4:12, Paul speaks of the "equipping of the saints for the work of ministry, for the edifying of the body of Christ." I grew up thinking all ministries were only in the church building. I had a paradigm shift fifteen years ago. I now understand that in order to have true Kingdom vision, we must see that the church also functions in the workplace.

I avoid international ministry through the church because their message is limited by their own vision. I knew the church would confine me, and there is more to ministry than just preaching sermons.

Traditionally, ministry has only been seen in the pulpit. Dr. Wagner explains it so well, that ministry includes not only the nuclear church, but the extended church as well, which makes up about eighty percent of the ministries. According to Ephesians 4:12 (NLT), "Their [the fivefold ministers'] responsibility is to equip God's people to do his work and build up the church, the body of Christ." Yes, work was ordained by God. It is a service to God and people. Work is a part of our worship, our service to God. It is time to activate sons and daughters in the workplace in this era.

CHAPTER 6

THE GREAT TRANSFER OF WEALTH

Wealth is often marked by an abundance of resources. Wealth is the nature of God. He is a God of abundance, a God of unlimited resources. Wealth can be in the form of financial windfall, such as inheritance, lottery, or a lucrative business deal.

When the people of God are empowered financially, they can easily pursue their God-given ambitions, goals, and purposes. Wealth brings freedom that helps many to fulfill their God-given assignments on earth. This includes dreams and aspirations that cannot be fulfilled if there is a lack of money.

The Bible has several passages that address wealth. The first example is when God transferred His wealth to Abraham (Genesis 12:7-10). Abraham was given the opportunity to inherit a huge land inheritance from his father, but he chose to give it all away to follow God to the land that He, God, would show him. Abraham's faith in God was so sincere that God rewarded him with a far greater inheritance that was fulfilled in part when his own offspring, the children of Israel, returned to the promised land of Canaan.

In Deuteronomy 8:1-2 (NIV), Moses tells the Israelites,

> "Be careful to follow every command I am giving you today, so that you may live and increase and may enter and possess the land the Lord promised on oath to your ancestors. Remember how the Lord your God led you all the way in the wilderness these forty years, to humble and test you in order to know what was in your heart, whether or not you would keep his commands. God is ready to release enormous, unprecedented amounts of wealth for the purpose of the advancement of His kingdom here on earth."

Proverbs 13:22 (KJV) states, "A good man leaveth an inheritance to his children's children: and the wealth of the sinner is laid up for the just." Also, in Isaiah 60:4–5 (NKJV), we read:

> "Lift up your eyes all around, and see: they all gather together, they come to you; your sons shall come from afar, and your daughters shall be nursed at your side. Then you shall see and become radiant, and your heart shall swell with joy; because the abundance of the sea shall be turned to you, the wealth of the Gentiles [nations] shall come to you."

One of the hallmarks of coming into agreement with a spirit of poverty is when we believe and think less highly of ourselves than how God sees us. For example, when Moses is at the burning bush, and God says (paraphrased), "I have a big job for you," and Moses counters, "you obviously don't know me." God saw Moses in one way, and Moses just couldn't go there. The poverty spirit makes you believe the lie that you don't have the means to be what God wants you to be.

Our portion is in the King Himself, and His inheritance here on the earth. Because we are made in God's image, and because the Spirit of Jesus dwells within us, we are more than able to do the good things he has called us to do.

In contrast to the purposefulness of wealth, poverty is money without an assignment. If you have it, you do not have to spend it. The scripture teaches that we are created in the image and likeness of God, implying that our lifestyle ought to reflect God to others. Our actions and behaviors should mirror the image and likeness of God to the world. This concept alone should deeply challenge and inspire you.

In this section, we will focus on one specific aspect of God's likeness that we should be reflecting upon—His abundance. It is stated in the Bible that God is plentifully wealthy.

Wealth is described as "an abundance of valuable resources" in the Scriptures.

WEALTH TRANSFER

God calls mankind to stewardship. God commanded Adam to take dominion. Our mandate is to establish a government on earth as if it is in heaven. We listen for our marching orders, then execute them.

> "Then God said, 'Let Us make man in Our image, according to Our likeness; let them have dominion over the fish of the sea, over the birds of the air, and over the cattle, over all the earth and over every creeping thing that creeps on the earth.'" (Genesis 1:26-28, NKJV)

With so much wealth multiplication happening in the market, the Marketplace Apostles who "serve as leaders, established apart from others, building a business, and leading it" (Wagner) demonstrate what wealth transfer looks like. Marketplace Apostles are visionary Kingdom leaders that engage in the concept of economic trade, and influence society beyond the four walls of the church. The marketplace is primarily where the children of God take the wealth of sinners and transfer it to the Kingdom of God.

We also see that the wealth transfer has not yet fully manifested. This is the reason Wagner cites Proverbs 13:22 (NKJV), "A good man leaveth an inheritance to his children's children: and the wealth of the sinner is laid up for the just." We are to work in God's blessings so that we may have enough to leave to our children and grandchildren with an inheritance of abundance.

Let us carefully note this distinction: that "the wealth of the wicked is stored up for the *just*"–not exclusively for the Christians! There has long been an expectation that the wealth of the wicked is stored up for the Christians, and at some point, in the near future, Christians will be blessed with vast wealth. Yet, this is not what Solomon stated when he wrote this Proverb.

Another aspect of wealth transfer is also for the children of God to exercise the abundance of their God- given authority and dominion Remember, we are all seated together in the heavenly places with Jesus (Ephesians 2:6), where like-minded Marketplace Apostles–entrepreneurial sons and daughters–are willing to learn through Kingdom insight, and serve as society leaders. The spiritual gift of apostleship in the marketplace has significantly impacted the exercising of authority and dominion in business culture. We are seated together in the heavenly places with Jesus, where like-minded entrepreneurs learn through the Kingdom's insight to serve society.

As someone once said, "We should try to be the best for the world." We, the marketplace believers, have learned to build altars, going before God with our living sacrifices of time. This reminds me of Romans 12:1, where it states that we are living sacrifices, and the good work that we do in the marketplace is part of our being living sacrifices offered to God, which includes our time, talents, and resources, where we download heaven's new strategies, and learn how to execute them to serve God's purposes for the nations. His wisdom is the best resource for bringing about different business solutions.

We become the Kingdom resource the world is searching for. As we evolve with our Heavenly Father, learning to adapt to change reignites the fire within us to transform any atmosphere, we operate in accordance with His Kingdom principles, and use wisdom through creativity to acquire resources and wealth. The Marketplace Ekklesia movement has become a bridge between the Kingdom and the world.

We have also seen glimpses of the eradication of the Babylonian economy, which is founded in pride and self-promotion, and causes social distresses of greed, fear, corruption, and self-centeredness. This can include issues like poverty, homelessness, unemployment, starvation, trafficking, substance abuse, domestic violence, family breakdown, unsustainable debt, suicide, slavery, radicalization, abortion, unfunded liabilities, and other similar issues.

We have seen different organizations replace all these social dilemmas with a Kingdom culture of caring and sharing, which leads to universal prosperity and human flourishing. These changes lead a nation to have an ideal preferred economy and to worship the one true God. I know we are not fully there yet, but I can see a huge shift in the marketplace, where true leaders are demonstrating how the Kingdom of God should look on the earth.

Our current generation is moving beyond mere citizenship of earth, and is beginning to invest life resources into learning the loyal ambassadorial roles of Kingdom sonship and daughtership as citizens of heaven. We can serve with integrity, dignity, and class, as children of God. God is shaping a new wineskin (Matthew 9:17) in the marketplace.

The idea and practices of being a one-man show is diminishing in the Kingdom as resources from a successful Kingdom Marketplace business are advancing us all. The leaders are understanding and walking in the creativity of heaven. There is so much life of God in the marketplace.

KINGDOM CONCEPT OF GIVING

God has unlimited resources, and our giving flows out of His abundance. Proverbs 3:9-10 says, "Honor the Lord with your possessions, and with the first fruits of all your increase; so, your barns will be filled with plenty, and your vats will overflow with new wine." First fruits offerings remind us that God is the source of *all* blessings! Giving God the first fruits of our harvest is a sincere act of devotion that establishes a spiritual exchange in the realm of divine beings. It demonstrates the belief that giving the best of your lambs to God will cause your flocks to prosper, and also demonstrates an expectation and trust in God's generous and abundant provision.

Offering first fruits is an act of faith which results in the multiplication of blessings into the heavenly realm, and is a gesture of love to God. The first fruits offering was the offering of the literal first fruits that were ripe at the beginning of the harvest season. First fruits should be given willingly from the heart, while tithing is a gesture of obedience. Essentially, giving first fruits is about initiating a transaction with the divine realm before anything else.

Giving is a celebrated act driven by creativity, and not just from a sense of duty, responsibility, command, or requirement. We see in Matthew 6:1-4, God was trying to correct an abuse of giving, prayer, and fasting. The focus is the motive. It illustrates that our giving should be done secretly, but also publicly, as mentioned in Acts 4 where believers had all their possessions in common, and there were no poor among them. This is to test us fully and to ensure that giving is being done the right way. The act of giving has different dynamics. We cannot just use one verse to practice giving and expect to cure the issues with our financial systems. God has designed us to grow in the act of giving, to find what works and does not work, by knowing Biblical principles and how to apply them.

Malachi 3:10 is the best-known verse in scripture right after John 3:16. As soon as somebody gets saved they're taught to tithe with the verse,

> "Bring the whole tithe into the storehouse, so that there may be food in my house. Test me in this," says the Lord Almighty, "and see if I will not throw open the floodgates of heaven and pour out so much blessing that there will not be room enough to store it." (Malachi 3:10, NIV)

We commonly encounter these two ways of thinking: one is that you are absolutely guaranteed financial blessings if you tithe, and the second is that you must tithe to the local church. I think many people have not seen a lifetime of results from tithing.

Many of us have spent years not tithing, and then have felt that God directed us to tithe and have seen immediate financial results from tithing. Many people have tithed for a season, stopped tithing, and they have seen immediate negative consequences from not tithing. Many sincere, obedient believers have tithed for years and have seen absolutely no benefiting impact in their finances. We do not see this mixed practice of tithing admitted in many churches, and yet it is public knowledge there are literally thousands and thousands of people who have listened to preaching on Malachi 3:10.

Some believers have tithed faithfully, sacrificially, and obediently by faith, and they have still seen absolutely no financial benefits. We see that some have even gone into actual bankruptcy while they have still been faithfully tithing. Tithing is not a one-step cure for financial problems.

When reading the Bible, it's important to read the entire passage to understand the context of individual verses in the passage. We want to understand this verse from

Malachi in its proper context. There are other sins listed throughout the whole book of Malachi. This list in God's word may include other possible causes for financial problems and a blocking of blessings. 1) Mechanical, uninspired worship by the priest (Malachi 2:2); 2) Judicial injustice (Malachi 2:9); 3) Divorce (Malachi 2:11); 4) Slandering God (Malachi 2:17); 5) Sorcery, adultery, perjury, and predatory business practices (Malachi 3:5); and 6) Robbing God of tithes (Malachi 3:8). Malachi 2 highlights that we can be under a curse and also under a blessing simultaneously. Malachi 2:1 (NKJV) says,

> "'And now, O priests, this commandment is for you. If you will not hear, and if you will not take it to heart, to give glory to My name,' says the Lord of hosts, 'I will send a curse upon you, and I will curse your blessings. Yes, I have cursed them already, because you do not take it to heart.'"

Through these various passages, we see that it is evident that there is no one-step solution to solving our financial problems. One purpose of tithing is to remove the consequences of curses that come from wrong behavior. You can live under blessings and curses. Malachi 3:10 is true because you are blessed, and yet the curses devour the blessings before they ever get to you, and so you never see them. It is even more difficult to dispute from this passage that one hundred percent of the tithe should go to the local church.

I would like to look at all of the passages of scripture that talk about tithing because there are not that many. There are extremely different pictures portrayed in all the scriptures. When we put these seemingly incongruent pieces of the puzzle together, we'll get a sense of the big picture regarding God's heart when it comes to generosity and giving.

The priests and other leaders of Malachi's time failed to live according to God's instruction which they were to teach to the people They weren't walking their talk. In the second chapter of Malachi, there are numerous accusations against their hypocrisy: treachery in the home, profanity in the sanctuary, mixed marriages, rampant divorce, and false teaching (Malachi 2:10-17).

God expects leaders to embody the life that their followers should live. Effective leaders understand that they must first exemplify a Godly, desired lifestyle. People imitate what they see, so leaders should be modeling righteous living before they serve as ministers, mentors, or managers. Notice what happened when Israel's leaders failed to live model lives: They failed to preserve truth for the people (Malachi 2:7), they diluted the people's appetite for growth and instruction (Malachi 2:7), they caused many to stumble due to their poor example (Malachi 2:8), they corrupted the covenant God made with them (Malachi 2:8), and they lost their credibility (Malachi 2:9).

TITHING

The first reference to tithing is Genesis 14:20, which is referenced later in Hebrews 7:1-10. It is the story of Abraham and Melchizedek. Abraham paid tithes to Melchizedek after returning from rescuing his nephew. We see there is no explanation in the text for why he tithed on this particular event, or how he arrived at the amount of ten percent. This is primarily a prophetic act which is later elaborated upon in Hebrews, where it also points out how Christ is so much greater than the law. Leviticus 27:30-33 says that there are two types—all the crops, and all the animals.

That presents a very interesting bookkeeping problem. Giving ten percent of all of the harvested crops for the year may be simple, but what about the animals?

Every year, shepherds were to take all of their animals up to the road and give every tenth animal to the Lord. Most of us do not raise animals these days, but this is what would be the equivalent of our capital—our money that makes money, just as sheep have the ability to reproduce and make more sheep. Does this mean we should give ten percent of the value of our house every year, ten percent of our equity, and ten percent of the value of the equipment in our companies?

It is an interesting problem, and one that is not often discussed on this subject. If we really want to tithe the Biblical way, we need to wrap our arms around this issue and figure out how to properly pay a tithe of our assets every year.

In Numbers 18:25-32, it says that the Levites were to take a tithe of what they received from the Israelites and give it to the priests, and they were to give a tithe of the best, not just any old ten percent. Deuteronomy 12:17-19 is the first passage that rocks the boat of a popular catchphrase spoken in many Christian circles, and it says that the Israelites are to eat their tithes in a selected city. They were not to eat it in their hometown, but they were to take it to the city that God would designate—which eventually was Jerusalem—and to eat their tithes there.

In case you are wondering exactly why they would be eating their tithes instead of giving them to the priests, God elaborates in great detail. Repeated passages expand upon the idea, not just in this one verse in Malachi. Also, in Deuteronomy 14:22-28 (NLT) it explains,

"You must set aside a tithe of your crops—one-tenth of all the crops you harvest each year. Bring this tithe to the designated place of worship—the place the LORD your God chooses for his name to be honored—and eat it there in his presence. This applies to your tithes of grain, new wine, olive oil, and the firstborn males of your flocks and herds. Doing this will teach you always to fear the LORD your God. Now when the LORD your God blesses you with a good harvest, the place of worship he chooses for his name to be honored might be too far for you to bring the tithe. If so, you may sell the tithe portion of your crops and herds, put the money in a pouch, and go to the place the LORD your God has chosen. When you arrive, you may use the money to buy any kind of food you want—cattle, sheep, goats, wine, or other alcoholic drinks. Then feast there in the presence of the LORD your God and celebrate with your household. And do not neglect the Levites in your town, for they will receive no allotment of land among you. At the end of every third year, bring the entire tithe of that year's harvest and store it in the nearest town. Give it to the Levites, who will receive no allotment of land among you, as well as to the foreigners living among you, the orphans, and the widows in your towns, so they can eat and be satisfied. Then the LORD your God will bless you in all your work."

Very simply put, two years out of three, you were to spend the entire tithe on yourself—the entire tithe on a huge party in Jerusalem, where you and your family would live it up, staying in the best hotel, eating filet mignon rather than living in poverty flats, eating at McDonald's. The third-year tithe was to be spent on the Levites, the foreigners, the fatherless, and the windows in their own towns. Deuteronomy 26:12-15 (NLT) reinforces that,

"Every third year you must offer a special tithe of your crops. In this year of the special tithe, you must give your tithes to the Levites, foreigners, orphans, and widows, so that they will have enough to eat in your towns. Then you must declare in the presence of the Lord your God, "I have taken the sacred gift from my house and have given it to the Levites, foreigners, orphans, and widows, just as you commanded me. I have not violated or forgotten any of your commands. I have not eaten any of it while in mourning; I have not handled it while I was ceremonially unclean; and I have not offered any of it to the dead. I have obeyed the Lord my God and have done everything you commanded me. Now look down from your holy dwelling place in heaven and bless your people Israel and the land you swore to our ancestors to give us—a land flowing with milk and honey."

The teaching is very clear that only one year out of three were the tithes given away. Two years out of three, a man and his family were to eat it themselves. The next passage to consider, Chronicles 31:5, is about the restoration of tithes and offerings to support the priesthood after a long period of neglect.

In Nehemiah 10, we have a repetition of this again after the Babylonian exile, when the people reaffirmed their covenant to give all the tithes and offerings that were due. In Nehemiah 12:44, we find the first real addition to the practice of the law, when the Levites began to forcibly collect the tithes at the appropriate times. They would go out to the field and collect in a location that seemed to be pragmatic. This practice was an addition given by the ruler Nehemiah, and was not part of God's original law.

In Amos chapter 4:4 (NIV), we have another statement—this is our third statement now about only one third of the tithes being given away. It says, "Go to Bethel and sin; go to Gilgal and sin yet more. Bring your sacrifices every morning and your tithes every three years." In three references in the New Testament, each one is not teaching the tithe, but it is mocking the tithe as a tool of orthodoxy.

In Luke 18:12 it says that the Pharisees would fast twice a week and tithe everything. In Matthew 23:23 it says the teachers of the law and the Pharisees go so far as to even tithe from their spices, but they neglect the law, justice, mercy, and faith. Luke 11:42 says they tithe the spices and omit justice and the love of God. So, in the New Testament, God absolutely refuses to accept tithing alone as a status of legitimacy. He is much more concerned about the holiness of our walk rather than whether we meticulously tithe the small things.

We cannot take one portion of the law and say it is binding to the New Testament saints while abandoning the rest. If you do not follow the dietary commands, if you do not follow the sacrifices, or you do not follow the feasts, why can you legitimately extract that one command of the tithe and apply to the New Testament Church, when there is simply no mention of the tithe in Acts or in any of the Epistles? Secondly, we cannot take one verse and ignore the other four passages that say that two-thirds of the time, the tithe is supposed to be spent on you and your household, and only one third of the time is it to be given away.

There is a flagrant lack of integrity in ignoring these passages, and many ministers have not touched on this portion of the topic, which is found in Deuteronomy 12, 14, and 26, and Amos 4. Instead, they focus only on Malachi 3:10.

The church has not preached on tithing according to the *whole* counsel of the word of God. So, my challenge is for church ministers to stop saying that tithing will fix all your financial problems, because that is not true, according to what is written in Malachi. There is an intentional twisting of the context of Malachi because there is no Biblical basis for saying that ten percent of the money of believers is supposed to be brought to a religious institution.

There are legitimate lessons to be learned from the Old Testament economy. Two-thirds of the Old Testament tithe was available to the Israelite family to be used and enjoyed in extravagant and abundant worship of thanksgiving to a good God who generously provides all things.

Let us now apply that in light of our own spiritual walk. Think about the potential of investing two-thirds of your tithes into your own spiritual edification. I know a man who takes each of his children to Israel when they turn a particular age—it is a rite of passage for them. I'm happy for him and glad that he has the money to do that.

What would happen if we had the funds to be able to do something extravagant as a rite of passage for each of our children? Or, at a particular age, what would happen if we use the tithe to take a couple of weeks off, to be alone with the Lord, and spend time with Him in a cabin in the woods? What would happen if we hosted a family reunion in the context of worship rather than just for the sake of frivolity, and used our tithe for that? God designed the Old Testament tithe to help Israelite families worship with joy and anticipation of the continued pouring out of God's abundant blessings.

A second lesson from Old Testament economy is for one-third of the tithes to be distributed by the Israelites to the Levites and to the poor, the foreigners, the widows, and the orphans. The Israelite heads of their households were responsible for making the difficult decisions as to who would receive what amount in the distribution of their tithe. This involved a whole lot of value judgments on the part of the individual rather than simply giving into a blind formula.

The option existed to give all of it to the Levites, and have them distribute it, but the expectation was that most of the Israelite men would distribute the tithe themselves. They would determine which poor person, which alien, which widow, which orphan, and which Levi merited their gifts.

Making decisions about giving is a huge responsibility. It is very different from a formula where you calculate a number and then put a check in the offering plate.

Here is another lesson: We notice that there is clear repetition in the different passages of giving to the marginalized and those who, in their culture, would not have been able to earn a substantial living on their own. God was very concerned that these minorities in Israel would receive financial help when they needed it. What would be the impact that America would have if one-third of the annual income of all the churches were invested in making restitution to the minorities who have been wronged? Now that would certainly change American history.

A third lesson is that God valued personal and relational responsibility in giving more than formulaic giving. Even for those two years when they were allowed to spend all of it on themselves and their family, there was a very overt push towards responsibility.

According to God's word, it was legally permissible to follow the formula that for two years, the tithe was for them and their families, and one year was for others; but they were also reminded to remember the Levites even in those two years of using the tithe on themselves. They were to be sure that the Levites did not go without—and there was no exact formula for how much you had to give to the Levites. God was encouraging personal responsibility for fellow citizens to look around and see which Levite had a family that needed some extra help.

Finally, God expected the religious leaders to live on the voluntary gifts of their fellow Israelites. Here in America, there is a certain amount of tension between churches and the Church movement. The simple reality is that most churches are not working in the trenches. Most churches are not getting dirt under their fingernails. Most churches exist to educate the saved, not to heal the broken.

Many parachurch groups are deeply involved in meeting the needs of orphans, widows, and foreigners. That is what God intended, and God saw to it that most of the time, the tithe went to the local needs of the people—it did not go to Jerusalem. It went to the orphans, widows, and foreigners, and to the Levites who were teaching at the grassroots level.

Even if the Jewish people gave all of their third-year tithe to the Levites, the Levites only gave ten percent of that to the temple in Jerusalem. Aside from those mandated tithes, everything else came from voluntary offerings given by the people.

God held the religious leaders responsible for the effectiveness of their ministry. When the temple of Jerusalem and the Levites in the field were effective in their ministry, the people would want to support them.

However, the people would not want to support them if they were not effective in their ministry. God had absolutely no safety net. God was perfectly content to allow ineffective spiritual leaders to starve. That is the brutal reality of the Old Testament system. Those are the four major passages in scripture containing the major concepts on tithing that have been seriously warped by popular doctrines.

THE NEW PARADIGM OF GIVING

This paradigm represents new ways for the modern-day Christian to give. I believe that, as New Testament Christians, we will be held responsible for the return on investment from our giving. Getting a good return on our investment for God requires a high level of creativity and skills. Let us look at Luke 19:11, the parable of the ten servants. One servant brought back the original capital fund untouched, another returned fivefold, and still another one got tenfold.

Understand that parables are distinct from illustrations. Parables, by definition, are an explanation of the principles of God's Kingdom. They are different from the Old Testament-the Old testament narratives were more historical or prophetic in nature, while in the New Testament parables told by Jesus were everyday life stories, and beyond any question of doubt, He commended the individual in the parable who received the larger return on his investment. It was not just a question of one person getting five and the other doing nothing, and it was not merely a comparison between good and bad.

The parable absolutely shows a comparison between good and better, and shows that God expresses His approval and appreciation for the person who did a better job of investing the funds that they were given.

The central focus of the passage was personal responsibility bathed in creativity. All ten men had an equal opportunity, and all started with the same capital. Yet one outperformed the others in an identical market, and God affirmed the creativity and the skill of the person who got a higher return on investment of his funds. Take 1 Timothy 5:17-18 (NIV), for instance. In it, it states,

> "The elders who direct the affairs of the church well are worthy of double honor, especially those whose work is preaching and teaching. For Scripture says, 'Do not muzzle an ox while it is treading out the grain,' and 'The worker deserves his wages.'"

Again, this reinforces God's principles for giving and generosity rather than giving a direct formula. This is expressed in the same way as it is in the Old Testament where the people were advised to not neglect the Levites. God looks at his peoples' creativity, skills, and knowledge, and sees how they deal with a situation.

In the Old Testament, both leaders and followers could contribute toward a mutual goal. For example, because Levites did not own land or have flocks to tend, they were able to spend their time serving in the Temple, or performing religious duties so that the community would become more godly, have better crops, and be able to give better offerings.

Similarly, because Levites spend their time ministering and blessing the community, landowners had more time to tend flocks and fields so they could contribute financially to the Levites. God now wants people in the pew to take a similar responsibility to judge what would be adequate compensation for the skills and needs of ministry leaders, and support them accordingly.

Consider the impact it would have on our spiritual communities if we were to invest in nurturing our pastors' spiritual walk. Imagine if your pastor could spend one day with someone like Bill Johnson, Heidi Baker, Todd White, or Benny Hinn. It would certainly take time and effort to make the arrangements, to find somebody within their network who would be able to reach out to them to request a day of their time to mentor your pastor, and they may need to be flown in from a long distance to meet with him. How valuable would it be for a congregation to invest into something like this for their pastors? This is the kind of creative ideas that God is looking for to get a higher return on investment. What would it take for you to pour into your pastor that would cause him to become a better man?

Or consider a less expensive investment: What would happen if you provided your pastor with an IT service person for three hours a month? For those who may not know, an IT service person is an information technology expert who understands computers. He or she could sit down with your pastor to work out all those little software glitches, and perhaps teach him how to operate different computer programs a little bit better. How much time could be saved with a simple gift of three hours a month for help with those pesky technological problems?

What would happen if you did maintenance on his home for him if he is not able to? Are there doorknobs that do not quite work? Are there faucets that leak? Is there a hose bib that needs to be changed? If you have great skill in those areas, and he has none, what would it do for him and his family if you were to help him with these things? How greatly would it benefit him if you were to creatively assess his need and take the responsibility for fixing his house or his car, or maybe even his garden?

The way we support our pastors does not have to be limited to money. Money is the least creative way of meeting a need, and God is calling us to a new level of responsibility, and to use our skills and creativity, and to steward our finances. There are many ways to creatively assess needs and prioritize volunteering our time and our skills over just giving monetary support.

1 Timothy 5:16 shows us that God wants us to make helping the poor one of our primary targets. He does not want us to misuse funds by alienating those in need. In both the Old and New Testaments God establishes a focus on personal responsibility which is supported by utilizing skills and creativity to address the needs of ministers and impoverished or marginalized members of the community.

God wanted local control instead of standardized administration. Local control is where people in the church volunteer to help other people in the church, while standardized administration is when individuals give money to the church and allows the church leadership to allocate funds to help either the pastors or the needy. The best form of local control is to have one person assessing or asking the needs of people in the neighborhood, and coming up with creative ways to meet those needs on a personal basis.

HOW IS WEALTH TRANSFERRED?

Giving through tithing is one example of how wealth is transferred to those in need. Another example is when God transferred His wealth to Jacob:

> "Then Jacob made a vow, saying, 'If God will be with me, and keep me in this way that I am going, and give me bread to eat and clothing to put on, so that I come back to my father's house in peace, then the Lord shall be my God. And this stone which I have set as a pillar shall be God's house, and of all that You give me I will surely give a tenth to You." (Genesis 28:20-22, NKJV)

Jacob was struggling to survive after he fled from his brother Esau who had vowed to kill him for tricking their father Isaac into giving him the blessing of the firstborn. God miraculously provided him with an unexpected inheritance that put him back on his feet and allowed him to marry into a powerful family.

We see that in both cases, in tithing to the marginalized and in building the wealth of Jacob, God was using wealth transfer as a demonstration of His nature: He is the God of abundance. By giving away His wealth, God was demonstrating that His Kingdom has unlimited resources. He will never leave nor forsake anyone who trusts in Him. God owns much, and it is His nature to bless His children.

The term "great transfer of wealth" was first used by political economist Thomas Piketty to describe the transfer of economic resources from the poor to the rich over a period of three decades. It is generally defined as a period of sustained economic inequality. Opponents of the great transfer of wealth argue that it has led to rises in economic inequality and poverty, and that it should be addressed through policy changes to reverse it. Wealth transfer will depend on individual cases. However, there are a few key reasons why it's important to reverse this poor-to-rich wealth transfer.

First, wealth transfer from the wealthy to the poor, which is known as equity wealth transfer, can help individuals maintain a comfortable standard of living into retirement. For example, if an individual has a large amount of wealth, they may be able to live quite comfortably into retirement without having to rely on the government pension system or other forms of welfare.

Second, equity wealth transfer can also help to ensure that individuals are able to pass on an inheritance to their children or other family members. For example, if an individual has a large amount of wealth, they may be able to help their children start their own businesses, or gain access to financial resources that they would not be able to access on their own.

Finally, equity wealth transfer can also help to reduce poverty and inequality in society. It's helpful for individuals to have a working understanding of the principle of multiplication of money. As Dr. Sunday Adelaja stated in his book, *Money Won't Make You Rich: God's Principles for True Wealth, Prosperity and Success,*

> "It is better and more lucrative to know how to create money than how to service it. The person who only knows what to do with money is at the mercy of those who know how to make and how to manage it."

CREATING WEALTH

There are many ways to create wealth, but the most common way is to start a business. Wealth is generated through the accumulation of assets (such as money, property, or business interests) or through the generation of income (such as through employment, entrepreneurship, or investment). However, it is unclear how much of a role luck plays in generating wealth.

Having worked in the marketplace for over twenty years, I have compiled a list of many ways for people to generate wealth. Methods can vary depending on skills and interests. Here are a few examples:

1. *Start a business*: This is perhaps the simplest way to generate wealth, as it allows you to control your own destiny and generate income. There are many options available, from small businesses to online ventures.
2. *Invest*: investing your money in stocks, bonds, and other assets can offer you the potential for steady growth over time. It can also be a way to get exposure to different industries and opportunities, so be sure to consult with a financial advisor to get the most out of your investments.

3. *Start a personal finance blog*: a personal finance blog can be a great way to teach people about financial planning and the principle of allowing money to work for you, and to learn from others who have experience with the topic. Blogging can be an easy way to make money.

Adelaja explained,

> "All of this is to say that people who are smart and really rich do not work for money. No, they make their money work for them. They do not have to work, because their money works for them through wise investments."

A study shows that baby boomers are set to pass to their children more than $68 trillion. They are responsible for the biggest increase in wealth in American history. "It's a generation that has accumulated a greater percentage of wealth than any other generation ever has," said Mark Mirsberger, a certified public accountant, and CEO of Dana Investment Advisors. There is no doubt that baby boomers have made huge contributions to our current economy and society.

A good example is when companies buy another company. This is referred to as mergers, acquisitions, or takeovers. My own company has experienced the acquisition of several other companies that were merged into our own.

We were involved in an intensive audit to decide whether or not it would be a good fit for both companies to merge. We have seen the company grow and improve technology operations. We have added more contracts, which means more revenue, and improved prospects in the market.

Passages in the Bible instruct us to be content, but contentment does not mean lack of pursuit or laziness. Jesus says we need to continue to do business until He returns, or until we go to be with Him. There is the admonition to give. The more I have, the more I give.

We are not to be greedy or covetous, nor deceive others or be unethical. "Dishonest money dwindles away, but whoever gathers money little by little makes it grow" (Proverbs 13:11, NIV) Adelaja says, "Millionaires understand the true nature of money as a force to be dominated, subdued, and directed for good. They know money is a good servant but a bad master, and they never allow it to rule or guide their work lives."

We are instructed to work hard and to not be lazy or sluggards. Proverbs 10:4 (NIV) tells us, "Lazy hands make for poverty, but diligent hands bring wealth." Rest and do everything from the seat of rest. Think of Jesus walking on the raging waves that were threatening to capsize the boat. He had supernatural peace during the storm that surpasses our understanding. It's God's desire for His children to live from this place of rest.

Adelaja gives a statement, "Stability, peace of mind, and joy in the family are far more important than money." Another charge is to follow the guidance of God so that you can plan ahead. "The plans of the diligent lead to profit as surely as haste leads to poverty." (Proverbs 21:5, NIV); and "Wise people think before they act; fools don't—and even brag about their foolishness." (Proverbs 13:16, NLT)

The principle of wealth is in alignment with the knowledge and wisdom of God. Kingdom-wealthy sons and daughters build their wealth, expand their ventures, and do not live in scarcity. Self-interest does not leave us better off. It does not work, and has never worked. Instead, we learn to walk in the supernatural power of God, trusting him and not man.

Nations were created to trade on many levels, distributing heaven's wealth to advance God's Kingdom. When we work hard, there is always an overflow to be made. With that overflow we can then trade beyond our work. God's principles work in the marketplace.

WEALTH TRANSFER AND THE CHURCH

There could be a number of reasons why the Church has not yet seen the great transfer of wealth, or experienced an increase in its wealth. One reason could be that the Church does not currently have the right business model or the right strategies to achieve this. Another reason could be that the Church is not fighting hard enough for its interests in the marketplace. Finally, it could be that the Church lacks the right talent to bring about these changes.

There are many reasons why the Church has not seen the great transfer of wealth. First, the Church is not a business and is not beholden to economic realities.

For example, the Church has not invested in the stock market, or sought to increase its wealth through mining or other commercial endeavors. Second, the Church is not beholden to the laws of the land. For example, the US church is exempt from paying taxes by declaring itself a nonprofit organization. Finally, the Church benefits from the power of persuasion and its ability to mobilize members to support its goals. Therefore, the Church is not as susceptible to economic forces as other entities.

Chuck Pierce of Glory of Zion Ministries stated that: "God is saying to us in this hour that He is ready to give us keys. These keys will unlock the supply we need to advance His covenant purposes." Pierce goes on to say that, in order for us to receive and use the keys, we must identify the "illegal domination of demonic structures from region to region" and then recognize that "apostolic authority must be established in a field if we are to reap the harvest in that field."

The Marketplace Apostles will lead the way to the great transfer of wealth. They are the catalyst that will make the best decisions regarding the wealth coming to the Kingdom. They have been prepared to navigate the changes, distress, and crisis of our time. They understand the challenges and opportunities. They will guide those in the Church through different stages of the coming wealth. This also aligns with a word Peter Wagner had shared in one of his books: "God has placed true apostles throughout the marketplace." They have been hidden, but we are in the season where we will see the powerful anointing, they've been given by God for this hour effectively penetrating darkness for the Kingdom of God.

Peter Wagner has given us great strategies for renewing our hearts and minds to be fully immersed in God's purposes here on earth. Wealth transfer is one of the most important concepts that we need to renew our minds. We are often faced with circumstances that could reinforce our negative beliefs about money. But by transferring some of our wealth to others, we can create a habit of thinking positively about money.

God's value system is focused on our posterity and the prosperity of our descendants, rather than where most of mankind's values are focused—namely on balance sheets, personal wealth, and power over others.

If we place our value in assets instead of aligning with God's value system, there will be serious economic and social consequences for our nation, for ourselves, for our children, and for their children after them. What account will we give when we stand before the Lord one day and explain how we conducted our business?

Solomon wrote the first 29 chapters in Proverbs, including Proverbs 13. Although the book of Proverbs itself was composed in the 7th century B.C., Solomon wrote these chapters in the 10th century B.C. These Biblical marketplace principles caused whole regions and whole nations to prosper because they applied God's methods to their trading or their business activities. They had a broader view in their minds of creating just economies, which in turn are the basis of sheep nations, which are mentioned in Mathew 25, and Isaiah 58:3-8.

A sheep nation is a community or people group that are incredibly generous and compassionate and whose kindness knows no bounds. They had a bigger picture in mind–one that went beyond just obtaining their own personal wealth, and as a result this led to universal prosperity and human flourishing in their communities while the rest of the world plunged into poverty.

Boaz named his son Obed after what he himself was doing—worshiping the Lord through service and obedience. The name Obed means "servant of God" or "worshiper." Obed would have learned this principle from his father, and he would have passed it down to his own son, Jesse, who incidentally was a wealthy, influential, and very wise civil leader. Jesse would have passed it down to David. David was a great king, strategist, military general, and a man after God's own heart.

David followed suit and did exactly as Boaz did, and he passed this knowledge down to his son Solomon. This is evidenced when he specifically told Solomon to consult the Lord and ask him for wisdom, and then apply this wisdom for Godly economic growth to the whole nation. So, from Boaz who was practicing these principles on a local level, this principle had come all the way down through the same family to Solomon, who executed them on a national level.

As his father David instructed, Solomon asked the Lord how to rule the nation of Israel the right way. The Lord gave him wisdom, and he applied that wisdom along with the physical wealth David had given him. Solomon went on to deal with corruption, greed, and self-centeredness. Remember that one of the issues he dealt with was the corrupt, lying, stealing of a woman who had stolen another woman's baby in I Kings 3:16-28?

David gave Solomon what today would be the equivalent of over three-hundred-thousand dollars' worth of gold and silver to build the temple and establish Israel as a sheep nation. This amount would have been as much as present day Israel's current GDP. Solomon was also given bronze, iron, special timber, jewels, and ivory. David also gave him the plans for the temple and other infrastructures. David trained all the workmen and told them to come under Solomon's project management. The businesspeople were trained to be involved.

David sat Solomon down and told him that, when God contacts him, he must ask for wisdom to govern the people. What an inheritance! This was what Solomon was referring to in the first part of Proverbs 13:22 (NKJV), "A good man leaves an inheritance to his children's children." Solomon created so much prosperity and so many jobs that unemployment amongst the Jews was zero, homelessness was zero, national debt was zero, and everybody, including neighboring nations, prospered.

"The Invisible Hand" is a phrase coined by Adam Smith, a famous Scottish economist who advocated for less government intervention and more market influence in the economy. Jesus's Biblical genealogy can be traced all the way back to Solomon. They were the same family—the Messianic line. Once we get saved, we become a part of this family—the family of God (Romans 8:15-17). Therefore, in order to prosper our communities and create human flourishing, we must understand how to conduct business God's way.

Wealth is a covenant blessing from God (Proverbs 10:22). Rewards for obedience (Deuteronomy 7:12-13), rewards for wisdom (Proverbs 8:18,21), and wealth and possession (material and spiritual) give honor and distinction to a person. Being wealthy will help people unlock and experience God in all levels of favor.

God is the owner of all wealth, and we are stewards of the portion of wealth He entrusts to us. Great leaders are only stewards of God's resources. Those who are good stewards multiply what God gives them. They seek God's guidance and wisdom concerning wealth. When sons and daughters of God are financially empowered, they easily steward God's provision. They prosper in spirit, soul, and body. There is no worry. Instead, there is freedom.

When we implement practical strategies, adopt a spirit of abundance, discern our giving disciplines, create wealth through investment, and use Biblical principles of economy, we the Church will be positioned to help facilitate The Great Transfer of Wealth, which will lead to the greatest harvest of souls the world has ever seen.

It is time for us to explore with the Father, knowing that, as ambassadors of the Kingdom, we are fully funded, protected, and reinforced by the authority of heaven to complete our assignments on earth.

CHAPTER 7

STRATEGIC SPIRITUAL MAPPING IN THE BUSINESS MOUNTAIN

WHAT IS SPIRITUAL MAPPING?

Spiritual mapping is defined as the practice of identifying the spiritual conditions at work in specific locations. This can include communities, cities, or nations. Rebecca Greenwood talks about this in her book, *Authority to Tread: A Practical Guide for Strategic-Level Spiritual Warfare*. Spiritual mapping requires research and discernment to identify the spiritual dynamics of a specific geographic area. Once the information is gathered, put together, and laid out, we can get a clearer sense of the spiritual condition of any given location. The aim is to understand the spiritual condition of communities or cities, identify strongholds and areas of spiritual need, and then develop strategic prayers and actions to bring about transformation and spiritual revival to those places.

Adeoye Olufemi's definition of spiritual mapping in his book, *Territorial Powers and Spiritual Mapping* is distinct from some of the other definitions: "It is a discipline of diagnosis, research tools, which discuss the obstacles to revival, growth, the spread of the Gospel and the move of God." He goes on to say,

> "What an X-ray is to a physician is what spiritual mapping is to the intercessor or evangelist so that they will not be wasting their effort. Spiritual geography and mapping can be described as seeing a city, a town, community, or region from God's perspective."

The Mountain of Business is important because, without finances, none of the other mountains can grow and flourish. When finances are abundant, it creates a stable culture which leads to a market and economic system that is free to pursue buying and selling. This commerce becomes the backbone of a nation. The negative impact is when we lack righteous leaders in this mountain, and we see corruption through idolatry, greed, and covetousness.

It is God's heavenly system that the Father has entrusted sons and daughters to govern. A nation, state, or city's health can be determined in part by the growth, health, and wealth of its economy. The Church must learn to raise faithful stewards who work together in unity, employing Kingdom economic strategies, and working together as a team to achieve the goal of ruling the Mountain of Business. "The

Lord will command the blessing on you in your storehouses and in all to which you set your hand, and He will bless you in the land which the Lord your God is giving you." (Deuteronomy 28:8, NKJV)

In Genesis 1:26-28, God gave man stewardship over His creation when He commanded Adam to take dominion. Our mandate is to establish a government on earth as it is in heaven.

In the Old Testament, the word for marketplace was "the gate," which is the public square where people met and did their business together. God has given us the earth with a vast diversity of resources.

Suppose the sons and daughters of God do not occupy the marketplace. Who will steward God's resources? He continues to say, "The silver is mine, and the gold is mine." Gold and silver are products of the earth God created. Go occupy those places He has called you to until He comes again. Shine your light in darkness. If we do not occupy these places, people who do not honor God will dominate in those influential places.

When there is a global crisis there is an opportunity for Ekklesia to be the salt of the earth. Marketplace Ekklesia is the bridge between the Kingdom and the world. They are the light of the world. The Father, Jesus, and the Holy Spirit are our best prototypes for redefining how we are to properly exercise leadership in the Marketplace. Here are some of the great characteristics of Christians in the marketplace that As Ken Eldred points out:

"Businesses are not Christian. People can be Christian; businesses cannot. Thus, the discussion centers around the characteristics of Christians in business, not about the characteristics of Christian businesses. It is a subtle yet important distinction. People can have right standing and communion with God, businesses cannot. People can be indwelt by the Spirit of God, businesses cannot. People can become sons and daughters of God, businesses cannot. Confusion about this can lead to questionable business decisions. Some people might seek to establish a Christian company by only hiring Christians. But how are they going to be salt and light in the workplace if they are surrounded only by fellow Christians?"

STRATEGIC SPIRITUAL MAPPING

In today's rapidly changing marketplace, it has become crucial for organizations to adopt holistic approaches for transformation. While strategic planning and operational efficiency are vital, considering the spiritual attributes of businesses can yield significant benefits. By integrating prayer walking, intercessory group prayer, and other relevant actions into organizational strategies, businesses can tap into spiritual resources and create an environment conducive to growth and success.

Strategic spiritual mapping in the workplace involves the identification and understanding of spiritual dynamics affecting an organization's operations. It recognizes that businesses are not isolated entities that only function in the natural realm, but are interconnected with the spiritual realm, which can significantly influence their outcomes.

Spiritual mapping helps leaders gain insights into the spiritual challenges and potential opportunities that exist within their business environments. By acknowledging and addressing these spiritual elements, companies can unlock hidden potential, enhance overall well-being, and foster a culture of faith, purpose, and alignment among employees.

STRATEGIES FOR SPIRITUAL MAPPING

Below, we will examine the ten strategies for spiritual mapping and discuss their application in the marketplace:

Bible Study and Character Development Classes

Engaging in Bible study, both individually during quiet times and as a group, is a key component of a formal approach to spirituality. It is important to spend time with each other studying God's word because it creates an environment of camaraderie, collaboration, and friendship. Setting aside moments for quiet reflection, living according to Biblical principles by demon-strating behavior that aligns with the values of the gospel, and actively serving others and performing acts of kindness and good works, are essential for developing good character.

Furthermore, maintaining attitudes of humility, generosity, genuine concern for others, and cultivating the fruits of the Spirit as listed in Galatians 5:22-23, which are love, joy, peace, patience, kindness, goodness, faithfulness, gentleness, and self-control, are crucial. Conversely, following a spiritual path also means leaving behind worldly ways and embracing a new mindset and lifestyle.

Scripture extensively discusses the contrast between the ways of the Spirit and the ways of sinful nature, urging followers of Jesus to adopt the former and abandon the latter (Romans 8:1-17; Galatians 5:1, 13-21; Ephesians 4:25-32; 5:1-20). However, it is important to note that embarking on this new journey is not seen as a sacrifice, but as a joyful, liberating, and privileged choice. Those who deeply follow Jesus aspire, as Paul suggests, to become more Christlike, and live in a manner that reflects the essence of the gospel of Jesus. (Philippians 1:27-28)

Prayer Walking

Prayer walking is a powerful spiritual exercise that involves silently moving throughout the business premises while praying, observing the surrounding scenery, and inviting God's presence, guidance, and blessings into that place. It serves as a means to engage with the presence of God and consecrate the physical spaces occupied by the organization to Him. The process is typically conducted by individuals or groups of believers who pray while walking through key areas such as offices, conference rooms, production areas, and even areas surrounding the business premises. The following steps can be incorporated into implementing a plan for prayer walking:

1. *Preparation:* Develop a detailed prayer walking schedule that includes specific areas to be covered during each session. Promote participation by informing employees about the purpose and significance of prayer walking.

2. *Training:* Conduct training sessions to equip employees with understanding about the power of corporate prayer, techniques for prayer walking, and guidelines for maintaining a respectful and non-disruptive presence in the workplace.

3. *Execution*: Divide employees into smaller intercessory groups and assign designated times for prayer walking sessions. Encourage participants to pray for the company's vision, mission, co-workers, clients, and any specific needs that may arise during the process.

Intercessory Group Prayer

Intercessory group prayer involves individuals coming together in a dedicated space to pray for the specific needs and challenges faced by the organization. Intercessors have a unique position. They are called to be near the throne of God, to hear His heart, and to stand on behalf of others. They are to occupy this position from a place of love, unity, grace, mercy, and humility. Intercession is war! It ebbs and flows. There are times when intercessors really feel the heat of battle, and the corporate prayer room seems very intense, loud, demanding, and pushy. After all, scripture reminds us that the violent take the Kingdom by force (Matt. 11:12)!

But nevertheless, warfare through loud and intense vocalization is not the way every prayer session should be handled. I believe that effective, sincere corporate prayer should reveal all the attributes of God—His gentleness, His tender mercy, unity, His unconditional love, and burden for the lost, and divine wisdom and intervention.

Implementing intercessory group prayer into a strategic spiritual mapping plan includes some of the following steps:

1. *Establish a Prayer Team:* Identify and select individuals with a strong spiritual foundation and a

heart for intercessory prayer. Define their roles, responsibilities, and commitment expectations within the team.

2. *Regular Meetings:* Organize regular prayer meetings either in-person or virtual, where the Prayer Team comes together to lift up the organization's concerns, goals, and challenges in prayer. A safe space should be provided for employees to confidentially share their petitions.

3. *Focused Areas:* Develop a rotating schedule to focus on different aspects of the business in each prayer meeting, such as leadership, employees, customers, financial health, and organizational growth. Encourage the team to seek guidance from scriptures and other spiritual resources.

4. *Prayer Requests:* Establish a system to collect prayer requests from all employees and actively address those concerns during intercessory group prayers. Maintain transparency and communicate insights, testimonies, and answered prayers to encourage participation and faith-building.

The spiritual gift of intercessory prayer in the market-place is a precious blessing for individuals led by the Holy Spirit. It is an invaluable gift that allows believers to intercede on behalf of their coworkers and on behalf of the organization, invoking God's will regarding strategies and direction. For those who walk in this gift of intercessory prayer, it is not only of benefit to themselves, but it will also have a positive impact on the workplace environment, and for those who work within it.

The marketplace can be a challenging place, but through the gift of intercessory prayer, individuals can overcome obstacles and bring transformation. Intercessors are skilled in seeking divine wisdom to address difficult situations, becoming channels of God's grace in the workplace.

This gift fosters a nurturing spirit of unity and collaboration among coworkers. Through their prayers, intercessors are able to create an atmosphere of harmony and peace. Additionally, intercessory prayer leads to spiritual growth, personal transformation, and a sense of purpose in the workplace.

During times of crisis, intercessory prayer in the marketplace brings about spiritual transformation in the lives of individuals. Through their prayers, people are drawn closer to God and experience His grace and love in their lives. Their prayers become a source of peace and stability in the midst of chaos. Moreover, intercession equips individuals with insights and solutions to overcome challenges. By seeking God's wisdom, intercessors are able to tap into divine knowledge that can offer creative and effective solutions to complex problems. This not only benefits individuals, but also the entire organization as it helps create a culture of innovation and resilience, and equips that organization to be capable of navigating through the toughest of times.

The gift of intercessory prayer in the marketplace has a profound effect in creating a spiritual climate in the workplace. As intercessors lift up prayers, they create an environment that is rich with God's tangible presence and power. This spiritual climate has the potential to influence coworkers and even transform the entire workplace culture and its leadership. Through prayer, the atmosphere becomes charged with positivity, love, and grace, resulting in increased morale, reduced conflicts, and an overall sense of well-being. The workplace becomes a haven where individuals can thrive, not only in their professional endeavors, but also in their spiritual walks.

In today's fast-paced and ever-changing world, the practice of intercessory prayer is often relegated to the confines of the sacred spaces of churches or spiritual retreats. However, an inherent gift lies within this divine act that extends far beyond the traditional boundaries of religious institutions. The marketplace, with its hustle and bustle, provides an untapped avenue for those with the spiritual gift of intercessory prayer to create a powerful impact on the lives of those around them.

The gift of intercessory prayer in the marketplace is not confined to sacred spaces, but can also have a profound impact on lives within the bustling environment of work. Embracing and utilizing this gift can lead to remarkable changes in individuals and organizations, promoting unity, growth, strength, and a positive work culture. Let us recognize and cultivate this gift to its fullest potential, and allow it to bring about transformative change in the marketplace. Incorporating prayer groups in business settings can potentially impact employee productivity and job satisfaction in several ways:

1. *Emotional well-being and stress reduction:* Prayer groups offer a supportive outlet for employees to share their concerns, burdens, and anxieties. Receiving prayer can be helpful for reducing stress levels, improving overall emotional well-being, and increasing job satisfaction and engagement.

2. *Enhanced morale and teamwork:* Prayer groups build a strong sense of community and collaboration among employees. Through prayer, God can grant patience to

employees to work together as a team, which helps create a supportive and inclusive environment. In turn, morale improves, teamwork is enhanced, and positivity is fostered in the work atmosphere, which leads to increased productivity.

3. *Increased focus and clarity:* Prayer and meditation enhances a contented mind, and can bring focus and clarity. Joshua 1:8 states, "This Book of the Law shall not depart from your mouth, but you shall meditate in it day and night, that you may observe to do according to all that is written in it. For then you will make your way prosperous, and then you will have good success." Good success is prospering in spirit, soul, and body. Prayer gives employees the opportunity to reflect, gain perspective, and prioritize their tasks and goals. This can lead to improved concentration, which helps when making well-informed decisions, and ultimately increases productivity.

4. *Strengthened relationships and reduced conflicts*: Regular prayer group meetings can lead to open and meaningful communication among employees. This can help build stronger relationships, soften our hearts, promote empathy, cheer hearts, and reduce conflict in

the workplace. Proverbs 15:1 says, "A soft answer turns away wrath." Favorable relationships create a harmonious work environment, and have a positive impact on job satisfaction and overall productivity.

5. *Encouragement and inspiration:* Sharing personal and professional struggles, challenges, and victories within the prayer group can uplift individuals and motivate them to overcome obstacles. This encouragement can boost morale, job satisfaction, and ultimately lead to increased productivity.

Implementing prayer groups in a business environment may also have potential challenges and drawbacks, which could impact employee productivity and job satisfaction:

Some of the drawbacks of incoporating prayer intercessor groups in business settings:

1. *Legal and diversity concerns:* In some businesses, promoting Christian spiritual activities in the workplace may raise legal concerns, particularly if it leads to discrimination or creates an exclusive work environment that disregards different religious or non-

religious beliefs. When considering the integration of prayer groups in a business setting, it is important for organizations to carefully assess the potential benefits and drawbacks, and to respect the diversity of their workforce, and ensure that everyone feels included and comfortable regardless of their beliefs or preferences.

The establishment of prayer groups in a workplace may raise concerns about inclusivity and diversity especially for non-Christian organizations.

If these groups are exclusively focused on a particular religion or faith, it may cause employees from different religious backgrounds to feel alienated, which could create a sense of exclusion and potentially impact job satisfaction. We should ask Holy Spirit for wisdom and strategies on how to be more inclusive while still maintaining the integrity of our faith.

2.   *Time management and productivity:* Engaging in prayer during work hours might disrupt employees' workflow and time management. If prayer groups are implemented as part of business strategy, there must be an appropriate balance between the busyness of

work where goals need to be met, and tasks need to be prioritized, and time spent meeting for prayer in a way that truly increases productivity and doesn't take away from it. Implementing structure into our daily lives helps establish a well-organized routine. If too much time during the workday is being allocated for each prayer, frequent interruptions for prayer sessions could lead to a decrease in productivity, missed deadlines, and increased stress levels for employees which could ultimately have a negative effect on job satisfaction.

3. *Religion is a sensitive topic:* Introducing prayer groups may create conflicts and divisions among employees. Differences in beliefs, religious practices, and opinions can create tensions that could lead to a lack of coherence within the team, which could also have a negative effect on overall productivity and job satisfaction.

4. *Perceived favoritism:* If management excessively sup-ports or promotes prayer groups, it may create a perception of favoritism toward a particular religious group. This can create resentment among employees who do not participate or belong to the same faith,

which could lead to decreased morale and job satisfaction.

5.   *Inclusion:* People may not want to be included because they don't feel safe sharing their challenges and struggles, be vulnerable with certain people, or be vulnerable in general. Sometimes there are people--Christians even--who believe themselves to be safe and Godly people, and want to pray for others. But in some cases, those people aren't as healthy as they believe themselves to be, and they end up over sharing those people's issues all around the office, and then there's embarrassment, shame, bro-ken trust, and all kinds of other potential conflicts and issues. It can be difficult for people to trust one another, because some people don't always have the best motives, even if they claim to be Christians. At worst, information offered during a prayer session could be used to mani-pulate or coerce, or be held against the employee that shared it. People are messy--even people with good intentions.

That said, I think that in a healthy context, and with healthy, mature Christian leaders, prayer / intercessor groups in the workplace have the potential to achieve everything as mentioned in the paragraphs above.

To mitigate the impacts on productivity and job satisfaction, businesses should consider:

1. *Promote an inclusive culture:* Encourage activities that celebrate diversity and accommodate employees of all faiths or beliefs.

2. *Provide optional spaces for religious activities:* Designating spaces where employees can engage in personal religious practices independently can help accommodate varying beliefs without affecting productivity.

3. *Ensure equal opportunities:* Avoid any form of preference or exclusion based on religion, and ensure fair treatment of all employees regardless of their beliefs.

4. *Open communication and respect:* Encourage open dia-logue about religious beliefs, ensuring that everyone's perspectives are heard and respected. Foster an environment where employees can express their concerns without fear of judgment or discrimination.

5. *Flexibility and balance:* Allow employees to maintain a work-life balance by accommodating reasonable requests for religious obligations while ensuring the overall productivity of the team.

6. *Optional participation:* Make prayer / intercessor group participation an option, but not a mandatory obligation or commitment. That way employees don't have to participate if they don't want to, but should feel welcomed, but not pressured either, or feel less valued just because they choose to abstain from joining the prayer group.

As a final point, the gift of intercessory prayer in the marketplace possesses great potential to significantly transform the workplace by enhancing peace, promoting wisdom, fostering well-being, and instilling hope. These benefits can render intercession an invaluable asset in today's fast-paced and demanding work environment. Intercessors, empowered by the Holy Spirit, are called on to release the power of prayer into the marketplace, and profoundly impact the lives of those around them, thereby revealing God's redemptive intentions.

In essence, the gift of intercessory prayer in the marketplace is an impactful tool that brings numerous advantages to individuals and to the workplace as a whole. Through their prayers, intercessors foster unity, personal and spiritual growth, offers support during difficult times, and cultivates a positive and transformative work environment. The significance of this gift cannot be underestimated as it holds the potential to bring about remarkable changes in the lives of individuals and organizations alike. Thus, acknowledging and nurturing this gift is crucial. We should allow it to be fully utilized to its maximum potential in the marketplace

Prophetic Session Strategies

In the fast-paced and ever-changing world of business, effective strategies are crucial for success. One strategy that is gaining attention and proving its worth is the prophetic session strategy. Prophetic sessions rely on tapping into intuition, foresight, and divine insights to make informed decisions and navigate challenges. While some may view this approach as esoteric or impractical, people who have practiced this strategy have found it to be beneficial and relevant to their businesses.

God is working through businesses in a whole new way. When you trade from heaven (celestial authority) first, your trading becomes natural because it is easy. You are building your business from heaven down. Receiving heaven's validation is the key to implementing strategies. Heaven provides the building blocks for your business. Prophetic sessions can provide guidance or validation on what steps to take to achieve certain goals, what products to add to your line, changes in strategy, or receive vision or mission for your business. Through prophetic sessions, we have the ability to see the completed business as it exists in the future, fully formed, and then we are tasked with reverse-engineering that vision of purpose back to this moment.

Strategies developed during prophetic sessions have the potential to provide valuable insight into the future. By using intuition and tapping into heaven, business leaders can gain a deeper understanding of industry trends, emerging markets, and potential stumbling blocks.

This strategy allows them to make more informed decisions and take proactive measures to seize opportunities and avoid pitfalls. In a business landscape where change is constant and competition is fierce, having a glimpse into the future can provide a significant advantage.

Furthermore, prophetic session strategies contribute to effective risk management. In business, risk is inherent, and successful enterprises are those that are adept at mitigating these risks. By incorporating prophetic sessions into risk assessment, businesses can identify potential threats before they occur, enabling them to develop proactive strategies to minimize their impact.

This approach reduces the likelihood of financial losses, reputation damage, and operational disruptions. Prophetic sessions offer a unique perspective on risk management that complements traditional methods and enhances overall business resilience.

Another crucial aspect of the prophetic sessions' strategy is its potential to foster innovation and creativity within organizations. By tapping into heavenly realm and with the help of Holy Spirit insights, business leaders can unlock new ideas, approaches, and solutions.

Conventional strategies often rely solely on data and analysis, leaving little room for creativity and out-of-the-box thinking. Prophetic sessions, on the other hand, encourage the exploration of uncharted territories, pushing businesses to think differently and explore unconventional ideas. This mindset shift can lead to breakthrough innovations, new product developments, and improved competitiveness in the market.

Lastly, the prophetic session approach helps foster a strong sense of purpose and authenticity within businesses. By aligning decisions and actions with a higher purpose, leaders can create a cohesive and united workforce. This sense of purpose inspires employees, instills a collective mission, and promotes an authentic company culture. In turn, this drives employee engagement, loyalty, and performance, and ultimately leads to increased productivity and profitability.

The importance of prophetic session strategies in businesses cannot be overstated. Through gaining insights into the future, determining effective risk management, fostering innovation and creativity, and cultivating a sense of purpose, businesses can thrive in today's competitive landscape. While some may view this approach with skepticism, the benefits it brings to organizations demonstrate its relevance and effectiveness. As business owners continue to navigate uncertainties and seek sustainable growth, integrating prophetic session strategies should be seriously considered as part of their arsenal for success.

Kingdom Leadership, Event-Empowerment, & Team Building Events

Leadership events for businesses have become increasingly important in today's ever-changing business environment. Conferences and seminars, which are popular leadership events, hold a significant role in the development and honing of skills needed for successful business leadership. These events not only provide valuable knowledge and insights, but also serve as a platform for networking and collaboration.

Attending leadership events offers a variety of benefits, including the opportunity to gain valuable knowledge and insights from industry experts and thought leaders. These events often have renowned speakers who have achieved great success in their respective fields. They share their experiences, offering valuable lessons and best practices that can be applied in different business contexts. By exposing participants to diverse perspectives and innovative ideas, leadership events help broaden their understanding of leadership, and encourage outside-the-box thinking.

Additionally, leadership events promote networking and collaboration among professionals from various industries and backgrounds. They provide a platform for like-minded indivi-duals to come together and exchange ideas, experiences, and challenges.

Building a strong network of peers and industry leaders is crucial for any business leader, as it opens doors to new opportunities, partnerships, and collaborations. These re-lationships can prove invaluable in terms of gaining insights, potential business leads, and even mentorship.

Another prominent advantage of leadership events is the opportunity to learn from real-life case studies. These events often include panel discussions or workshops where successful leaders share their personal journeys and the strategies, they use to overcome obstacles and achieve their goals. Such insights are invaluable for aspiring leaders as they offer practical advice that they can apply to their own managerial roles.

These case studies provide a rare opportunity to learn from the experiences of others without having to go through the same trial-and-error process.

Moreover, leadership events serve as a platform for self-reflection and self-development. The opportunity to step away from day-to-day operations and immerse oneself in a focused learning environment allows leaders to gain a fresh perspective on their own leadership style and identify areas for improvement. By attending workshops and participating in interactive sessions, leaders can refine their skills, learn new techniques, and enhance their decision-making abilities.

Leadership events provide numerous benefits to businesses and their leaders. The knowledge, insights, and experiences shared during these events help enhance leadership skills, foster collaboration, and inspire innovation.

Furthermore, networking opportunities and exposure to real-life case studies contribute to professional growth and development. By investing in leadership events, businesses can cultivate a culture of excellence and ensure their leaders are equipped with the necessary tools to navigate the complexities of today's business world.

Discipleship Programs

The concept of discipleship as derived from Jesus' teachings and assignment on earth has been adopted within the business context to emphasize the importance of mentorship, guidance, and continuous learning. Jesus charges:

> "Go therefore and make disciples of all the nations, baptizing them in the name of the Father and of the Son and of the Holy Spirit, teaching them to observe all things that I have commanded you; and lo, I am with you always, even to the end of the age." (Matthew 28:19-20)

Those who assist and teach the C-level (highest-ranking in an organization, executives, and managers), and other leaders have been chosen by Jesus to fulfill the task of spreading the Christian faith to all nations (Matthew 28:19-20; Acts 1:8; Isaiah 49:6). Initially, this task involves guiding and nurturing new, inexperienced, or indifferent believers, often referred to as young believers in Christ, and aiding in their spiritual growth and development.

This serves as the fundamental building block for all Business as Mission. The approaches employed to accomplish this are numerous, but ultimately it often relies on a more mature Christian who genuinely cares about the growth of the new believer, teaching them all aspects of the faith.

Business as a mission is successful when its reach is long-term and international and it creates opportunities for people to minister holistically in the name of Jesus to others in the workplace who are hurting, bringing them the truth of the gospel. Christ calls each of us to embark on a lifelong journey.

The process of discipleship is a maturation process, for which the writers of the New Testament, particularly Paul, provide comprehensive guidance. Without this growth, the new believer may likely decline and spiritually perish. However, through this growth, CEOs and management discover a newfound purpose and enthusiasm for life, both personally and professionally.

God's command in the Great Commission is explicit: Go and make disciples. Being a business owner and not a missionary does not excuse you from this command. You, too, have a responsibility to go and make disciples. Acton says that many business owners easily define their business as a "sandbox." This refers to the specific area in which they aim to excel. This includes factors such as geographic region of focus, distinguished products or services, and exceptional customer service.

However, Kingdom business owners often struggle to define a spiritual sandbox in which their company can have a dominant and impactful presence. Defining a spiritual sandbox is challenging because it is difficult to measure spiritual progress. Ultimately, it is God who works in this area. Consequently, many godly business leaders do not approach the type of spiritual impact they are suited for with strategic planning in mind.

The Apostle Paul had a clear spiritual sandbox. He knew that he was called to preach to the Gentiles. As you contemplate your role in the Great Commission, consider the sandbox in which God has summoned you to make disciples. Making disciples involves two things:

1. Assisting people in establishing a relationship with Jesus.
2. Teaching them to follow God's commands.

Which of these areas will you focus on? How will your company contribute to making an impact in its spiritual sandbox? Devoting strategic thought, resources, and evaluation to your spiritual sandbox is as important as doing the same for the rest of your business.

Discipleship programs are a comprehensive training initiative designed to develop, equip, inspire, and cultivate future or current emerging leaders for the marketplace, church, and society. These programs can incorporate both individual in-person mentoring as well as online mentoring service opportunities. Leaders would participate in practical scenarios that cultivate and utilize their talents, which will allow them to simultaneously acquire the skills needed to integrate a Christian perspective across all aspects of the businesses. By emphasizing principles of discipleship, organizations can create a supportive culture that focuses on the growth and development of their employees.

Commissioning Angels

When we engage heaven, the Lord reminds us that He is the Lord God. He is almighty and all-powerful. He is increasing and without an end, and He is King forever. He is Holy, beyond all, righteous, and true. Any witchcraft, occult, manifestations, evil trades, or cursing from those aligned with evil will not override the victorious King. We fight with certainty of His victory against evil. Sometimes, we are weak in the knowledge of our position in Christ Jesus, and we are burdened by overwhelming attacks of the enemy and spiritual arrows that try to pierce our confidence.

God desires for us to be diligent stewards with the time, talents, and resources He has given us to work with so that the casualties of warfare are minimal. Many in the army of the Lord need to co-labor with angels. They are mighty, capable, and work on our behalf. Angelic assistance is very important in doing spiritual warfare. Father has given us the chance to work together. The angels are yearning for this time to co-labor with us.

Angels are powerful, capable, and have abilities that humans do not possess. God wants us to put them to work to assist with our assignments here on earth.

Therefore, we must commission them more often. When we go to pray, we ought to strengthen ourselves with the ministry of angels. We can call them near to minister to us and for us. They will always work on the plans for the Kingdom. They will always accomplish the plans of our King.

We can commission angels to strengthen business believers to execute and carry out the heavenly blueprints, carry revelation, and penetrate areas with light where there is darkness. This assists businesspeople by widening the portals of revelation and bringing more protection against the enemy's plan.

Spiritual Trainings

Christianity is a life strategy that gives people of the world the principles of the Kingdom of God and dismantles anything that is not of His Kingdom.

In the marketplace, people are called to walk in integrity as Daniel walked with integrity and faithfulness to the Lord while he and his people were captives amidst their Persian and Babylonian captors, and keep the message of the Kingdom. They are to bring dignity and empowerment back to the world every day, Monday through Friday. Despite the challenges faced by believers in different religious marketplaces, they learn to birth ideas, strategies, products, and services through prayer rather than just waiting for things to happen.

The world comprises a vast variety of religions that are observed in different parts of the world. Well-known faiths such as Judaism, Islam, Buddhism, Hinduism, Confucianism, Baha'i, and Taoism all exist alongside numerous variations of other religious practices, including Protestantism, Catholicism, Christian Science, Orthodoxy, Mormonism, Unitarianism, Universalism, Scientology, and New Age, as well as organized secularists, atheists, Satan worshipers, Wicca, and Voodooists. Additionally, there are countless other spiritual groups, religions, sects, and cults globally, which have been present throughout history.

These various religious or spiritual groups each lay their claim on specific geographic territories, whether it is a home, neighborhood, city, nation, or land belonging to a particular group of people.

Christians have been entrusted by Jesus Christ with the mission of spreading His teachings to the entire world. Consequently, those who spread this message, whether they are traditional missionaries or nontraditional missionaries, like Business as Mission practitioners, are effectively entering territories claimed by these religious groups. They may face opposition, depending on the circumstances. In regions where multiple groups are established, their interactions can range from living and working together in relative harmony, to experiencing chronic conflict, or even engaging in open warfare.

CHAPTER 8

KINGDOM PRINCIPLES IN BUSINESS

WHAT IS KINGDOM?

The concept of the Kingdom refers to God's rule and reign over all the realms, both spiritual and physical, in which God reigns as King, and the fulfillment of His will on earth as it is in heaven. According to the Bible, the concept of the Kingdom is a central theme that runs throughout both the Old and New Testaments. The idea of the Kingdom is a complex and multifaceted one, and it encompasses the rule and reign of God, the establishment of a community of believers, and the promise of a perfected future in which God dwells with his people for eternity.

In the Old Testament, the concept of the Kingdom is closely tied to the idea of God's sovereignty over all creation. The Israelites understood that God wanted to be their king, and that they were to live in obedience to his laws and commandments. I wonder what Israel would have looked like if they had allowed God alone to be their king? This was God's original plan. But Israel wanted a man to be their king so they could be like the other nations. So, God gave them what they wanted, and built it into his plan of redemption.

The Kingdom of God was meant to be a manifestation of God's righteous rule on earth, a place where justice, peace, and harmony could flourish. Through the prophets, God promised to establish a Kingdom that would bring about the restoration and renewal of all creation, victory over sin, and would ultimately bring us back into intimate relationship with Him.

In the New Testament, Jesus brought a radical message of the Kingdom of God. He preached that the Kingdom was at hand, and that the fullness of it could be experienced here and now, not just in the future. Jesus' ministry was a demonstration of the Kingdom's power. He healed the sick, cast out demons, and proclaimed liberty to the oppressed. By doing so, Jesus was revealing that the Kingdom of God was breaking into the world, and that it could bring about transformation in people's hearts and lives.

The Apostle Paul also played a crucial role in shaping early Christian understanding of the Kingdom. Paul emphasized that the Kingdom of God was not just for the Jews, but for all people, regardless of their ethnic or social backgrounds. He taught that through Jesus' death and resurrection, the Kingdom had been inaugurated in a new and powerful way.

Paul also spoke of the future consummation of the Kingdom when Christ would return and establish his rule over all creation.

In the book of Revelation, the Kingdom is depicted as the ultimate fulfillment of God's plan for redemption and restoration. In the final chapters of Revelation, we see a vision of a new heaven and a new earth, where God will dwell with His people in a perfect and glorious Kingdom. This Kingdom is described as a place where there will be no more suffering, pain, or death; a place where God will wipe away every tear from our eyes, and where the redeemed will reign with Christ forever.

The concept of the Kingdom, according to the Bible, is rich and profound, and encompasses both the present and the future. It is a reality that transcends and brings transformation in both spiritual and physical realms, a place where God's rule and reign is acknowledged and embraced. The Kingdom of God is a promise of hope and restoration, a vision of a future in which all things will be made new. As believers, we are called to live in the light of this Kingdom right now.

KINGDOM PRINCIPLES

Kingdom principles serve as a blueprint for believers to live a life that is pleasing to God and that are in line with His Kingdom purposes. By applying these principles, believers are able to experience the blessings and fulfillment that come from living a life surrendered to God's will.

Every human being has problems that they are struggling to solve. Through God's wisdom, we have the solutions to those problems. We cannot expect Kingdom results if we are not applying Kingdom principles. Some practical ways in which believers engage with God to obtain answers to their problems. Each person's relationship with God is different, and so different people will experience Holy Spirit's revelation in different ways.

- Hear words of knowledge, word of wisdom, personal prophecy.
- See pictures in their minds, or things superimposed over physical reality.
- Receive confirmation through "coincidental" circumstances.
- Hear through scriptures. All scripture is given by inspiration of God.

As each believer grows in their relationship with God, they learn to better understand the special and personal ways God speaks to them.

Non-believers, such as Richard Branson, Bill Gates, and Warren Buffett may seem to experience blessings and success without serving God. The verse that's coming to mind: "God causes the rain to fall on the just and the unjust alike." (Matthew 5:45) There are also unbelievers who, because God's ways are intuitive to us because we are made in His image, that they follow Kingdom principles without even being aware that this is what they're doing.

I've also become more aware of ungodly gain, and that people are able to obtain power and wealth when they engage with the demonic. But this type of gain only leads to ungodly bondage that can only be broken by the redemptive power of the blood of Jesus. This is an intriguing, powerful question, as principles are for time, not for eternity. They have nothing to do with salvation, and they are universal. There is no Baptist electricity, Hindu electricity, or Muslim electricity. There's only electricity. These principles are applicable for everyone regardless of their faith in Jesus, or lack thereof.

The principles for success are available for everybody, and those who have become wealthy through wise business practices have absolutely tapped into God's principles even if they aren't seeking or acknowledging Him. My biggest challenge as a business consultant in the Christian and secular community is that believers often rely on faith as a substitute for best business practices, while non-believers diligently seek and apply these principles, which leads to their success. This contrast highlights the importance of understanding and implementing fundamental principles of business and success regardless of religious beliefs.

Believers will anoint their buildings with oil, pray and fast, but then violate so many basic business principles, and then wonder why God isn't blessing their business. It is important to apply best practices— "Practices 101"— because businesses are best stewarded when they are built utilizing basic, good business practices.

Some examples is where some Christians in business would prioritize profit over honesty and integrity when making any business deals. This leads to a poor reputation. Another area is where business may neglect the well- being of their employees. This can be seen in areas like providing safety, good benefits that is supportive their family, offering good income or even promoting a healthy work balance.

A few examples of good business practices people should be following when building their businesses. Integrate employee feedback in your business. The most valuable resource in a business is its workforce. The more you integrate. Recognizing employees for their good performance is a successful strategy for motivating them and build a positive company culture and workplace environment.

Believers often turn to God as a means of justifying poor business decisions, but this is not the ideal relationship that God wishes to have with His sons and daughters who are in the business world. Instead, God wants to guide and elevate businesspeople to a higher standard. There is a clear distinction between believers and non-believers, and God should not be held accountable for unethical or unwise actions of Christian businesspeople. It is a complex issue, but the truth is that non-believers often achieve great success due to their diligence in understanding and applying business principles, while believers sometimes take a more passive approach, relying only on prayer instead of best practices, which is not an effective substitute.

RELIGION VERSUS KINGDOM

The seductive power of religion lies in its capacity to act as a counterfeit substitute for the Kingdom and, as a result, can impede us from seeking true solutions to our predicaments. Through my examination of the essence of religion as compared to the Kingdom, I have discovered several important truths:

RELIGION	KINGDOM
Occupies and engages man pre-Kingdom	Fills man with core purpose
Prepares man to depart earth	Enables man to rule over earth domains
Man reaches up to God	God reaches down to man
Focuses on escaping earth	Focuses on impacting and transforming earth
Brings earth to heaven	Brings heaven to earth

In the Gospel of Matthew, Jesus explicitly addresses the religious leaders of his time. In chapter 23, verses 13-15 He condemns them for their hypocrisy and for hindering the Kingdom of God. He begins by saying, "But woe to you, scribes and Pharisees, hypocrites!" and then goes on to list the various ways in which they are neglecting the true heart of God's law and are leading others astray.

Jesus accuses the religious leaders of shutting the door of the Kingdom of Heaven in people's faces, using their knowledge and authority to keep others from entering. He labels them as hypocrites who are more concerned with outward appearances and the traditions of men rather than truly seeking God. He also criticizes them for their zeal in making converts, only to make them twice the child of hell as they are themselves.

Through these verses, Jesus addresses the religious spirit that values legalism and conformity over genuine relationship with God. He calls out the religious leaders for their pride, self-righteousness, and neglect of true justice, mercy, and faithfulness. Jesus's words serve as a warning for all who fall into the trap of religious legalism, reminding us that true righteousness comes from a heart surrendered to God, not from adherence to man-made rules and traditions. Religion serves as one of the greatest obstacles in the

Kingdom. This is a wake-up call to the church to abandon religion and come back to the Kingdom.

> "But woe to you, scribes and Pharisees, hypocrites! For you shut up the kingdom of heaven against men; for you neither go in yourselves, nor do you allow those who are entering to go in. Woe to you, scribes and Pharisees, hypocrites! For you devour widows' houses, and for a pretense make long prayers. Therefore, you will receive greater condemnation. Woe to you, scribes and Pharisees, hypocrites! For you travel land and sea to win one proselyte, and when he is won, you make him twice as much a son of hell as yourselves." (Matthew 23:13-15)

Jesus makes it clear in Matthew 5:20: "For I say to you, that unless your righteousness exceeds the righteousness of the scribes and Pharisees, you will by no means enter the kingdom of heaven."

KEY KINGDOM PRINCIPLES

The principles of integrity, compassion, stewardship, and ethical conduct are fundamental for any well-functioning society, organization, or individual. These key Kingdom principles are essential for fostering a balanced and prosperous community, and they form the basis for a harmonious and ethical existence.

Integrity, as a Kingdom principle, refers to the qualities of honesty, reliability, and strong ethical morality. It necessitates that individual be consistent in their actions, values, methods, measures, expectations, and outcomes. Integrity is the foundation upon which trust, and credibility are built.

In a Kingdom context, it is crucial for leaders at all levels to practice integrity as it sets the tone for the entire community. Through the practice of integrity, leaders and individuals demonstrate their commitment to upholding truth, fairness, and transparency, and they inspire others to follow suit. In doing so, they create a culture of trust and accountability, and they set the stage for a just and equitable society.

Compassion is another key Kingdom principle. Compassion is the ability to empathize with others and to act with kindness and understanding towards them. In a Kingdom setting, compassion is an essential element of creating a community that is inclusive, supportive, and caring. It involves recognizing the inherent worth and dignity of each individual, and it calls for a commitment to alleviating suffering and promoting the well-being of others.

Compassion fosters a sense of interconnectedness and solidarity, and it serves as a catalyst for fostering positive relationships and building a sense of common purpose. By practicing compassion, individuals and communities can work towards eradicating social injustices, and they can strive for a world where everyone is treated with respect and empathy.

Stewardship is the responsible management and care of resources and assets, and it is a key Kingdom principle that encompasses environmental, economic, and social responsibilities. In a Kingdom context, stewardship involves recognizing that all resources are gifts from the Creator, and as such, they should be managed and protected with wisdom and foresight. Stewardship includes practices that promote sustainability, conservation, and responsible consumption, and it requires a commitment to balance the needs of the present with the needs of future generations.

Moreover, stewardship extends to the promotion of social justice and equity, and it calls for an equitable distribution of resources and opportunities for all members of the community.

By embracing the principle of stewardship, individuals and communities can work towards a world that is characterized by ecological balance, economic justice, and social harmony. As leaders, we are entrusted with nothing less than the responsible stewardship of everything God owns and has entrusted to our care.

God has promised us that if we fulfill our responsibilities of integrity and good stewardship, He will receive abundant blessings. However, if we fail to do so by walking in disobedience, we allow ourselves to be vulnerable to the devourer to destroy what we produce. Leaders, especially those in high positions of authority, must remember that we do not own anything. We are simply managing God's resources.

Finally, ethical conduct is a key Kingdom principle that underscores the importance of upholding moral and ethical standards in all aspects of life. It calls for a commitment to honesty, fairness, and justice, and it requires individuals to act with integrity and respect for others.

Ethical conduct is essential for creating a community that is characterized by trust, accountability, and ethical decision-making. It involves making choices that are aligned with one's values and beliefs, and it requires individuals to consider the impact their actions have on others. By practicing ethical conduct, individuals and communities can work towards creating a society that is grounded in justice, mutual respect, and ethical leadership.

The key Kingdom principles of integrity, compassion, stewardship, and ethical conduct are essential for fostering a balanced and prosperous community. They provide a framework for creating a society that is characterized by trust, integrity, compassion, and ethical decision-making. By embracing these principles, individuals and communities can work towards a world that is characterized by justice, compassion, and social equity.

In today's business world, there is a growing trend among companies to integrate Kingdom principles into their operations. Kingdom principles are God's words that provide a framework for individuals to govern the Kingdom of God. These are ethical and moral values, and can include concepts such as compassion, stewardship, honesty, integrity, service to others, and leadership. Companies that embrace these principles often find that it leads to greater success, not only in terms of financial profits, but also in terms of employee morale and customer satisfaction. Below are a few examples of companies that have successfully integrated Kingdom principles into their operations.

Chick-fil-A is one of the most well-known examples of a company that has integrated Kingdom principles into its operations. The fast-food chain, founded by devout Christian S. Truett Cathy, is closed on Sundays to allow employees to attend church and spend time with their families. In addition to this commitment to faith, Chick-fil-A is also known for its strong customer service and commitment to ethical business practices, as well as creating quality dining experiences and delicious food for their customers.

The company is consistently ranked as one of the best places to work in the United States, and has a loyal customer base that appreciates its commitment to Christian values.

Patagonia, an outdoor clothing, and gear company is also known for its commitment to Kingdom principles. The company has a strong focus on environmental sustainability, and has made significant efforts to reduce its environmental impact and promote ethical sourcing and production practices. Patagonia's commitment to integrity and environmental stewardship has helped it build a loyal and socially conscious customer base that has established the company as a leader in the sustainable business movement.

These examples show the positive impact of integrating Kingdom principles into business operations. Companies that embrace compassion, honesty, integrity, and service to others often find that it leads to greater success and positive relationships with employees and customers.

By following these principles, companies can create a more ethical and sustainable business environment, and ultimately build stronger and more successful businesses.

WHEN FIVEFOLD DYNAMICS HELPED REVOLUTIONIZE AN INDUSTRY

— Walt Pilcher, author of The Five-fold Effect:
Unlocking Power Leadership for Amazing
Results in Your Organization

Here's a story from my days working at L'eggs® (the pantyhose in plastic eggs). It's an illustration of apostolic marketplace leadership, albeit serendipitous because at the time my colleagues and I had no practical knowledge of the five-fold leadership gifts of Ephesians 4:11-16 ("And He Himself gave some to be apostles, some prophets, some evangelists, and some pastors and teachers, for the equipping of the saints for the work of ministry, etc.").

We know that most people have more than one of the five-fold gifts, with one or possibly two often being much stronger than the others. Still, it can be surprising when someone you think has one predominant gift suddenly jumps into another one, if only for a season. Bill Caldwell is a good example. As Sales VP and an outstanding salesman, Bill had a critical role in the tremendous success of L'eggs, convincing practically all US supermarket, drugstore and discount chains and stores to carry our products. He was a true evangelist for the company. I was the Marketing VP, the apostle assigned to the marketing function, if you will. The Marketing and Sales departments had a cordial if sometimes tense relationship, mostly because, at least in those days, salespeople thought marketing people were out-of-touch ivory tower types (not entirely wrong), and marketing people had a culture of looking down their noses at the folks who had to deal with actual customers. But Bill and I liked each other, and he was highly respected for being very good at his job.

L'eggs brand was doing well: High quality hosiery with distinctive packaging, attractive pricing, broad distribution, effective advertising, an excellent reputation with retailers and consumers, and the leading market share by a wide margin. In other words, an excellent marketing program, thank you very much.

One day Bill said, "We should run some promotions to round out the advertising campaigns." We had distributed some cents-off coupons in our magazine ads but had never done any promoting beyond that, such as giving allowances to our retailers to offer special price reductions on certain products for limited time periods or sponsoring special events to draw attention to the brand, such as a women's 10K race.

"Why?" I asked. "We're doing great without spending money on promotions." I was of the "If it ain't broke, don't fix it" school and quite legalistic. Besides, what salespeople typically want, in unbridled evangelistic fashion, is just to spend all the company's money on frivolous pandering to the retailers who carry our products, right? Weren't the profit margins we were giving them good enough already?

Bill's argument was simple. "We're doing well, but why not see if we can do even better? Let's at least try it." Well, I couldn't disagree with that, so I decided to embrace it. Together we developed a promotion plan that we recommended to our boss the president, who approved it. The plan worked, sales and profits soared, and a culture of mutual respect, honor, and trust was formed between the Sales and the Marketing departments (and Bill and me) that impacted the culture of the rest of the company from that time onward, surviving several organization changes.

In five-fold terms, there was the top company evangelist sharing his prophetic wisdom! Bill saw an opportunity and became who he needed to be for the team at that time.

This and other instances of five-fold-like teamwork helped L'eggs revolutionize the women's hosiery industry, enhancing value and convenience for the consumer. We didn't know it then because we knew nothing in those days about the five-fold leadership plan of Ephesians 4:11-16, but we were enjoying a generous taste of what I like to call "the five-fold effect." It's fun to imagine the even greater success we might have seen if we had indeed known and applied with intentionality the principles of the five-fold plan.

These examples show the positive impact of integrating Kingdom principles into business operations. Companies that embrace compassion, honesty, integrity, and service to others often find that it leads to greater success and positive relationships with employees and customers.

By following these principles, companies can create a more ethical and sustainable business environment, and ultimately build stronger and more successful businesses.

The principles of integrity, compassion, stewardship, and ethical conduct are fundamental to the function of any society, organization, or individual. These key Kingdom principles are essential for fostering a balanced and prosperous community, and they form the basis for a harmonious and ethical existence.

---

[1] I was not the architect of the L'eggs marketing strategy, however. That distinction belongs to David E. Harrold, who began his marketing career at General Mills and then went to Hanes Corporation in Winston-Salem, NC, maker of the leading brand of women's hosiery for department stores. There he developed the revolutionary idea of selling quality women's hosiery through supermarkets and drugstores using a direct-to-store distribution system similar to bread and soft drinks instead of going through wholesalers or retailers' warehouses. He hired me as Marketing Manager to help take L'eggs into test market and national rollout. Eventually, I became Marketing VP and then President.

IMPACT OF KINGDOM PRINCIPLES ON BUSINESS

The Kingdom of God encompasses all areas of human activity, including politics, education, business, and the arts. Dr. Wagner argues that the Church, as the primary vehicle for advancing God's Kingdom, has a responsibility to bring about societal transformation and promote justice, righteousness, and peace in all spheres of life.

He emphasizes the need for believers to engage in prayer, intercession, and spiritual warfare to overcome the forces of darkness, and establish God's rule on earth. According to Wagner, the concept of Kingdom is a holistic and all-encompassing framework through which we understand and engage with the world. It is a call to bring about transformation and justice in all spheres of life, and to actively participate in advancing God's rule and reign on earth.

CHAPTER 9

KINGDOM LEADERSHIP

DEFINITION OF KINGDOM LEADERSHIP AND ITS TRANSFORMATIVE IMPACT

- A Kingdom leader is someone who recognizes the supreme authority of Christ and is submitted to that authority.

  Examples: David, Hezekiah

- A Kingdom leader takes discerned risks by sowing in new directions and in unplanted fields with the goal of bringing in an increase for the Kingdom.

  Examples: David, Solomon

- They are explicit and intentional in expanding the Kingdom by focusing on the areas that maximize his returns that grow the Kingdom in terms of resources, land, influence, and power.

  Examples: David, Solomon, Jehoshaphat

- A Kingdom leader recognizes his human limits, and develops his people by entrusting them and empowering them to take responsibility and ownership in the Kingdom they are growing in together. This is also known as a

Servant Leader.

Examples: Solomon, Hezekiah

- A true Kingdom leader has advisers everywhere, but understands that God has placed him in this position of authority. Thus, he makes all decisions at the throne of God.

(Examples: Solomon, Hezekiah).

CHAPTER 10

EXAMPLE OF A STRATEGIC MASTER BUSINESS AS MISSION

In the exciting journey of entrepreneurship, the genesis of a business plan is often viewed as the establishment of a blueprint from a beautiful blend of personal and spiritual inspiration. While some theologians may offer their interpretations, this unique process transcends conventional definitions. It is a personal experience of asking God and solving problems with Him. This what I call "the God talk process".

In my own experience, the emergence of my business blueprint was a profound revelation, distinctly rooted in my encounters with God in His presence. During a time of prayer and reflection, I sought clarity about my divine blueprint, and in that peaceful space, I felt a powerful call to action, using the God given blueprint which fueled my passion for entrepreneurship.

I encourage you to embrace your own journey with Him, and trust that those moments of connection as God's friend can lead to exciting new ventures! I wanted to include strategies from my own business plan in the pages ahead to give you some ideas for what your own business plan could look like.

IT Technology Consulting Company

The Strategic Master BAM Business Plan is a crucial element in the operations of our IT Technology Consulting Company.

STRATEGIC BUSINESS PLAN EXECUTIVE SUMMARY

Tech Kingdom IT Technology Consulting will be established as an information technology firm that specializes in marketing and tech Consulting of high-technology products in the Kenyan market which will target the African nations as potential clients. Its ownership base is composed of former information technology consultants, all of whom operate in the local industry. They are founding Tech Kingdom IT Technology Consulting to formalize the consulting services they provide.

OBJECTIVES

- Sales of $1,550,000 in year 1, and $3 million by year 2.
- Gross margins greater than 80 percent.
- Net income sustained at more than 10 percent of sales through year 2.

MISSION

Share your mission statement, your product or service, and basic information about your company's leadership team, employees, and location. You should also include financial information and high-level growth plans if you plan to ask for financing.

KEYS TO SUCCESS

1. Leveraging a wealth of knowledge of Information Technology, we are able to explore various avenues of generating revenue such as market research, published reports, project consulting, and retainer consulting.
2. Faith integration, Biblically based business principles, spiritual growth, social and economic impact.
3. Competency in visibility to establish new business leads.

4. Profitability, sustainability, financial independence, and transformation.
5. Trustworthy expertise, reliable, quality, confidential information.

COMPANY SUMMARY

Briefly share what your company is and why it will be successful. Example: Tech Kingdom IT Technology Consulting is a new firm with high-level expertise in high-tech marketing of IT resources, channel development, business development, and distribution strategies.

SERVICE DESCRIPTION

Describe what you sell, or what services you offer.
 Example: Tech Kingdom IT Technology Consulting first seeks to gain a comprehensive understanding of the client's organization's situations, constraints, and objectives.

COMPETITIVE COMPARISON

Research other companies that offer products or services that are similar to yours. Competitive analysis helps you understand what makes your business unique so that you'll know how to communicate those strategic differences to effectively market to your business's targeted demographic.

MARKET ANALYSIS SUMMARY

Your strategy should evolve and change to fit_current market trends, and the unique needs of your business's targeted demographic.

Business in the IT industry has progressed and has had a significant increase in profit margins over the last few decades as the global market continues to transition to digital platforms as a way of conducting business. The emergence of new technology solutions and the internet have had a momentous impact on how businesses is implemented for IT solutions.

Even with this progress, the industry still lacks the intellectual resources needed to guarantee effective transitions that guide new business ventures during this information era. The arrival of digital technology platforms has profoundly altered the structure of conventional business models. This affects how both businesses and non-profit organizations operate.

MARKET SEGMENTATION

- *Small Business Enterprises* – a rapidly expanding segment, this fragment is demarcated as small organizations usually owned by sole proprietors.
- *Ministries, churches, and community-based projects* – This segment is comprised of faith-based community organizations which are largely nonprofit.

TARGET MARKET SEGMENT STRATEGY

Understanding the target market is important for any business to craft effective marketing strategies. Businesses that prioritize marketing their services to a specific demographic of consumers are better equipped to be to be attentive in their concentrated marketing approach.

MARKET NEEDS

According to an article written in *Information Technology for Development* Magazine by P. K. Wamuyu, professionals in the IT consulting business have noted three diverse niches that exist in the industry.

1. *Temporary technical aid* – This area includes short-term assignments for providing solutions.
2. *Troubleshooting services*

3. *Specific skill* – The largest area is in software specialty, which encompasses system purchasing and setup services, system optimization, training, network administration, repairs, database development, disaster recovery, data storage, telecommunications, and data protection.

SERVICE BUSINESS ANALYSIS

An assessment of Tech Kingdom IT Technology Consulting's main competitors shows no overwhelming competition that could bar Tech Kingdom's success. Similarly, identifying our competitors' weaknesses illuminates key areas that Tech Kingdom can leverage its own marketing strategies.

BUYING PATTERNS AND COMPETITION

As illustrated above, the IT consulting industry is fragmented with varying specialties and sizes. Two key factors of competition are apparent in the industry. The main competitors seem to be clustered into two groups: those who offer consulting services for the products they sell, and those that provide network services to large organizations. Smaller organizations seem to favor large organizations as their ideal clients. Nonprofit organizations need these services to leverage job opportunities for their communities, and for economic and social growth.

STRATEGY AND IMPLEMENTATION

Tech Kingdom IT Technology Consulting will emphasize the following to grow and establish the organization:

- A comprehensive and detailed marketing strategy to capture new markets.
- A competitive edge founded on the cultivation of healthy relationships with customers.
- The value of offering practical and timely solutions at sound rates with a hundred percent satisfaction guarantee.
- Four key promotion approaches: referrals, networking, web-centered promotion, and conventional media marketing, as well as other non-conventional promotion approaches.

COMPETITIVE EDGE

Tech Kingdom IT Technology Consulting's competitive edge is based on the fact that the organization is founded on Kingdom principles and has competent professionals who are knowledgeable in various sectors including, but not limited to,

IT, marketing research, missions, leadership, and legal expertise. Experience in these areas will be essential for developing high-quality relationships with potential clients.

POSITIONING STRATEGY

Tech Kingdom IT Technology Consulting provides fast and effective responses that restore their organization's systems in operation. Compared to other competing firms in the industry, Tech Kingdom IT Technology Consulting offers a hundred percent satisfaction guarantee.

PROMOTION STRATEGY

The lead strategy implemented by Tech Kingdom IT Technology Consulting will be to emphasize cultivating healthy relationships with customers by using known networking approaches to gain recommendations and new client leads.

CHAPTER 11

TECH KINGDOM IT TECHNOLOGY CONSULTING BAM PLAN

Marketplace involvement has huge potential for taking holistic mission to every area of influence. It's incredible how operating in the marketplace gives us so many opportunities to indiscriminately meet and connect with a diverse community of people from all walks of life. Business is essential to any community.

As stated by C. Neal Johnson, "Businesspeople acting together in partnership with the local missionaries and churches can accomplish holistic mission in a way that none could accomplish alone." It not only met the real needs of hurting people, but gave them a sense of hope and a tangible understanding of the universal brotherhood of Christ."

Johnson also expressed that advocates of Business as Mission hold that business firms operating within local marketplaces represent innovative and critical avenues for benefiting economically and spiritually impoverished individuals with the gospel, and are an efficient approach to building healthy, reproducing communities.

Aching individuals around the country not only require immediate reprieve (this is well-accorded by Christian, secular, and non-profit organizations), but also long-lasting spiritual renewal and economic development.

Tech Kingdom IT Technology Consulting's effort to realize this transformation of individuals and communities is facilitated for the reason that the sphere of influence of this business initiative is not merely restricted to just their own employees—it also incorporates the investors, vendors, clients, and the communities with whom the organization will have a working relationship. We have the capacity to realize the holistic, transformational, and sustainable Kingdom impact on individuals who are deprived of such IT services around the country, and to build Christ's Kingdom which is encompassed by fair strategies that are outlined in Tech Kingdom's business plan.

THE BOTTOM LINES OF THE PLAN

THE SPIRITUAL BOTTOM LINE

Ultimately, the initiative of business as a mission cannot yield successful results unless employers are pointed to the redemptive power of Christ. Consequently, Tech Kingdom IT Technology Consulting will promote Kingdom business solutions, present its diversity, and take initiative in the (to quote Ken Eldred) "integration of work faith, economic development, spreading the gospel, transforming nations and transforming lives." It will continue to develop Kingdom values and principles among the untapped market.

Committed employers who exhibit the loving attitude of Christianity to other employees and aid the Holy Spirit to attract the lost to Christianity will be vital to the spiritual revitalization within the Tech Kingdom workforce and the community as well. Biblically based, God-honoring practices will be infused into all aspects of the business's mission.

Unsaved, marginalized, and individuals struggling with poverty need employment opportunities and hope. The Tech Kingdom plan will accord employment opportunities to community individuals which will bring hope and wealth creation.

ECONOMIC BOTTOM LINE

Economic prosperity denotes a priceless asset for any community setting. Profit is the lifeblood of any company, without this the venture dies. As mentioned by Eldred, profit reflects the value and quality of the services we offer.

The Tech Kingdom plan provides valuable information technology services and creates profitable and sustainable ventures. Accordingly, wage recipients with buying potential can help stimulate the local community economies and help better the living standards of surrounding communities. The positive out-growth of such job creation is demarcated by economists as what Brian W. Albright refers to as the "multiplier model."

CHAPTER 12

THE ROLE OF SOCIAL ENTREPRENEURSHIP IN NATION-BUILDING

Social entrepreneurship is a growing and important field that combines business acumen with a desire to create positive social change. It is often described as an innovative and sustainable approach to addressing societal problems and improving the well-being of people and communities. In this chapter we will explore the definition and characteristics of social entrepreneurship, highlighting the key elements that distinguish it from traditional entrepreneurship.

At its core, social entrepreneurship is driven by a mission to solve a social or environmental problem. This can take many forms, including addressing issues such as poverty, education, healthcare, environmental sustainability, and more. Unlike traditional entrepreneurship, which focuses primarily on financial returns, social entrepreneurship places equal emphasis on creating social value. This means that social entrepreneurs are not only concerned with making a profit, but also with making a positive impact on the world around them.

One of the key characteristics of social entrepreneurship is the use of innovative and creative solutions to address social challenges. Social entrepreneurs often leverage new technologies, missions, business models, and partnerships to develop sustainable and scalable solutions that can have a lasting impact on the environment and surrounding communities. Their approaches are often highly adaptable, and they are willing to take risks in order to achieve their social objectives.

Another defining characteristic of social entrepreneurship is the commitment to sustainability and long-term impact. Social entrepreneurs are not interested in quick fixes or temporary solutions. They are dedicated to creating lasting change that will endure beyond their own involvement. This often requires a focus on building the capacity of local communities, fostering leadership, and empowering the people they seek to serve.

Social entrepreneurship also emphasizes collaboration and partnerships as a key strategy for achieving social impact. Social entrepreneurs often work with a wide range of stakeholders, including government agencies, nonprofit organizations, businesses, and community organizations in order to leverage their collective expertise, resources, and networks. These collaborations help maximize the reach and effectiveness of their efforts, as well as build a stronger foundation for sustainable impact.

Social entrepreneurship is a dynamic and impactful approach to addressing complex social and environmental challenges. It is characterized by a strong mission-driven focus, innovative problem-solving, long-term sustainability, and collaborative partnerships. By harnessing the power of business and entrepreneurship, social entrepreneurs are driving positive social change and creating a better world for all.

SOCIAL ENTREPRENEURSHIP: NURTURING SUSTAINABLE CHANGE

Social entrepreneurship is the point of convergence between creative solutions and urgent societal problems. It is a potent strategy that utilizes the principles of conventional entrepreneurship to facilitate significant transformation and establish enduring effects. These individuals, commonly known as social entrepreneurs, are motivated by a twofold objective: to generate financial gains, and confront social or environmental difficulties.

THE THREE PILLARS OF SOCAL ENTREPRENEURSHIP

1. *The concept of innovation*: Social entrepreneurship involves the utilization of creativity and fresh ideas to devise effective solutions for intricate issues. This may encompass the development of cost-effective healthcare options for marginalized communities, or the creation of environmentally friendly technologies, which illustrates the pivotal role of innovation in their initiatives.

2. *Sustainability:* In contrast to conventional charitable models, social entrepreneurship places emphasis on long-term sustainability. The design of these ventures is carefully constructed to ensure financial viability, thereby securing the continuity and scalability of their positive impact over an extended period.

3. *Social impact*: The fundamental aim of social entrepreneurship is to facilitate positive social transformation. Whether it pertains to poverty alleviation, educational promotion, or climate change mitigation, these ventures are dedicated to generating tangible and quantifiable enhancements within society.

EXAMPLES OF SOCIAL ENTREPRENEURSHIP

The following are examples of Christian business owners who have put their faith into practice through their businesses and are now making a positive impact in the world.

Entrepreneur Blake Mycoskie is the founder of TOMS Shoes, a company that implements a one-for-one business model in which a pair of shoes is donated to a child in need for every pair sold. Mycoskie, who identifies as a Christian, is committed to using his business as a force for good in the world. The concept for TOMS Shoes originated from Mycoskie's visit to Argentina, where he was deeply moved by the poverty and lack of footwear among the children he encountered.

Consequently, he made the decision to establish a business that not only provides shoes to those in need, but also fosters job creation and sustainable economic growth in underprivileged communities. Mycoskie has frequently emphasized the influence of his faith on his work with TOMS Shoes, citing his Christian beliefs as the driving force behind his dedication to social justice and his aspiration to effect positive change globally. He views his involvement with the company as a means of embodying his faith through impactful action. This pioneering approach not only caters to a fundamental need, but also underscores the capacity of business to promote philanthropy.

Another example is Dave Ramsey, a well-known financial expert, and the creator of Ramsey Solutions. He is deeply committed to his Christian faith, and has based his company on Biblical principles. Ramsey has authored numerous extensive articles discussing how individuals can incorporate these principles into their personal finances. He advocates for individuals to steer clear of debt, live within their means, and prioritize saving for the future. Ramsey promotes debt-free lifestyles and judicious financial management. Additionally, he instructs his employees in a lifestyle of putting God first, and he actively supports Christian charities through his company.

James Cash Penney, also known as J.C. Penney, was an entrepreneur who founded the department store chain bearing his name. His Christian faith had a profound influence on both his personal life and his approach to business. Raised in a deeply religious family, Penney credited his father's strong faith as a formative influence, and often spoke about the role his own faith played in shaping his life and career. He viewed his success in business as a means of honoring God and serving others. Penney's commitment to service greatly impacted his leadership and achievements.

Penney was renowned for his dedication to his employees, emphasizing respect and providing opportunities for personal and professional growth. He established programs to support employee training and development, advocating for employees to live out their faith in the workplace. One of his most significant contributions to the community was the creation of the J.C. Penney Foundation, which supported a variety of cha-ritable causes, including education, healthcare, community development, as well as religious organizations and missionary work.

These stories illustrate the impact of faith in action. Many Christian business leaders leverage their success to make a positive difference in the world, whether through philanthropy, community service, or other initiatives.

This serves as a powerful example of how faith can be a force for good and inspire others to live out their values, and ha-ve a positive influence in their own businesses and communities. For Christian business leaders seeking to integrate their faith into their professional lives, consider exploring Convenes CEO Peer Groups, where members learn how to grow their businesses, become more profitable, apply God's Kingdom principles, and become culture-shapers.

IMPORTANCE OF CREATING SUSTANABLE SOLUTIONS TO ADDRESS SOCIETAL CHALLENGES

Social entrepreneurs have the capacity to create sustainable and innovative solutions that have a positive impact on individuals, communities, and the environment by applying Kingdom business principles to address social issues. Furthermore, these enterprises have the potential to generate employment opp-ortunities,-income,-and-foster-innovation.

CONCLUSION

God is breaking His people out of all the misconceptions that His work is only for spiritual leaders in ministry positions. Every type of work, either in the church building or outside the four walls of the church, is an opportunity to serve God, to serve others that He has assigned you to, to make a positive impact, and to be the light in the workplace in all capacities. Church and work are not two separate tasks, but rather both are ways of ministering.

Ephesians 4:28 highlights the importance of working hard and using our God given talents for the benefit of His Kingdom. In Corinthians 10:31, work is done with the intention of bringing glory to God. Proverbs 6:6-8, We have the responsibility to work.

Hear God's invitation to step into the field. It's time to cross over. Rise up like an Eagle. Become those who live the defining characteristics of everyone who is in God's covenant. Move from the old wine into the new wine. Let us shift our ways of thinking and allow God to make us into the fine work He originally intended us to be.

He has already opened new doors of opportunities for sons and daughters to walk in their futures. How we choose to see and think at our place of access is how the door will open up. Do not fear the new. Multiply it and steward it well. We have everything we need to walk in the new wine. Marketplace Kingdom leaders, the world needs what you have! Step forth and unpack! Unfold and release the DNA inside of you!

REFERENCES

Adelaja, S. (2016). *Money Won't Make You Rich: God's Principles for True Wealth, Prosperity and Success.*

Golden Pen Limited. Albright, B. W. (2014). *When Business is the Mission: A Study of Faith-Based Social Business in Sub-Saharan Africa.* Eastern University.

Eldred, K. (2005). *God is at Work.* Ventura, CA: Regal Books.

Glory of Zion Ministries. (2018). *Home.* https://gloryofzion.org/

Greenwood, R. (2005). *Authority to Tread: A Practical Guide for Strategic-Level Spiritual Warfare.* Grand Rapids MI: Chosen Books.

Johnson, C. N. (2009). *Business as Mission: A Comprehensive Guide to Theory and Practice.* InterVarsity Press.

Reggie McNeal, Reggie (2000). *A Work of Heart: Understanding How God Shapes Spiritual Leaders* New York, NY: Jossey-Bass Inc., A Wiley Company.

Olufemi, Adeoye A. (2023). *Territorial Powers and Spiritual Mapping.* Independent Publisher.

Park, Y. K. (2015). BAM Concepts in the Bible: Foundation from Original Words. *William Carey International Development Journal*, *4*(2), 29-36.

Shearer, D. (2021). *The Marketplace Christian: A Practical Guide to Using Your Spiritual Gifts in Business*. High Bridge Books LLC.

Silvoso, E. (2007). *Transformation: Change the Marketplace and You Change the World.* Chosen Books.

Silvoso, E. (2009). *Anointed for Business: How to Use Your Influence in the Marketplace to Change the World.* Bloomington, MN: Chosen Books.

Simmons, B. (2020). The Passion Translation: With Psalms, Proverbs, and Song of Songs. BroadStreet Publishing Group, LLC.

Wagner, C. P. (2006). *The Church in the Workplace*. Ventura, CA: Regal Books.

Wagner, C. P. (2012). *On Earth as it is in Heaven: Answer God's Call to Transform the World*. Minneapolis, MN: Chosen.

Wagner, C. P. (2013). *This Changes Everything: How God Can Transform Your Mind and Change Your Life*. Ventura, CA: Regal Books.

Wallnau, L. *Seven Mountains: The Rise and Fall of Nations* 2 DVDs and 2 CDs. www.lancewallnau.com.

Wamuyu, P. K. (2015). The Impact of Information and Communication Technology Adoption and Diffusion on Technology Entrepreneurship in Developing Countries: The Case of Kenya. *Information Technology for Development*, *21*(2), 253-280.